Your Intercultural *Marriage*

Your Intercultural *Marriage*

A GUIDE TO A HEALTHY, HAPPY RELATIONSHIP

MARLA ALUPOAICEI

MOODY PUBLISHERS

CHICAGO

All Scripture quotations, unless otherwise indicated, are taken from the *New American Standard Bible®*, Copyright ©1960, 1962, 1963, 1968, 1971, 1972, 1973, 1975, 1977, 1995 by The Lockman Foundation. Used by permission. (www.Lockman.org)

Scripture quotations marked THE MESSAGE are from *The Message*, copyright © by Eugene H. Peterson 1993, 1994, 1995. Used by permission of NavPress Publishing Group.

Scripture quotations marked NIV are taken from the *Holy Bible, New International Version®*. NIV®. Copyright © 1973, 1978, 1984 by International Bible Society. Used by permission of Zondervan. All rights reserved.

Quotations from *Intercultural Marriage: Promises & Pitfalls*, 3rd ed., by Dugan Romano, 2008, reprinted with permission of Intercultural Press, Boston, Massachusetts.

The poem "Uniquely Me" and the "Iceberg" diagram from *Third Culture Kids: The Experience of Growing Up Among Worlds* by David C. Pollock and Ruth E. Van Reken, 2001, reprinted with permission of Intercultural Press, Boston, Massachusetts.

All Web sites listed herein are accurate at the time of publication, but may change in the future or cease to exist. The listing of Web site references and resources does not imply publisher endorsement of the site's entire contents. Groups, corporations, and organizations are listed for informational purposes, and listing does not imply publisher endorsement of their activities.

Editor: Christopher Reese
Interior Design: Ragont Design
Cover Design: Smartt Guys design
Cover Image: iStockphoto
Author Photo: Tammy Labuda

Library of Congress Cataloging-in-Publication Data

Alupoaicei, Marla
 Your intercultural marriage : a guide to a healthy, happy relationship
/ Marla Alupoaicei.
      p. cm.
 Includes bibliographical references.
 ISBN 978-0-8024-1854-8
 1. Marriage--Religious aspects--Christianity. 2. Interethnic marriage.
 3. Intercountry marriage. I. Title.
 BV835.A457 2009
 248.8'44--dc22

                                    2009008586

We hope you enjoy this book from Moody Publishers. Our goal is to provide high-quality, thought-provoking books and products that connect truth to your real needs and challenges. For more information on other books and products written and produced from a biblical perspective, go to www.moodypublishers.com or write to:

Moody Publishers
820 N. LaSalle Boulevard
Chicago, IL 60610

1 3 5 7 9 10 8 6 4 2

Printed in the United States of America

To my darling husband, Catalin.
Your love has blessed my life.
Thanks for letting me share our story
so others may have hope.

Contents

[TAKING THE LEAP OF FAITH]

WITHOUT FAITH it is impossible to please [God], for he who comes to God must believe that He is and that He is a rewarder of those who seek Him.

By faith Abraham, when he was called, obeyed by going out to a place which he was to receive for an inheritance; and he went out, not knowing where he was going. By faith he lived as an alien in the land of promise, as in a foreign land . . . ; for he was looking for the city which has foundations, whose architect and builder is God.

[HEBREWS 11:6, 8–10]

In some ways, *every marriage is an intercultural marriage.* Perhaps you and your fiancé or spouse hail from two different countries. Perhaps you're of different races or ethnicities. Or maybe the two of you are simply from different cultures within the same country. For example, maybe one of you is from a large Italian family in New York, while the other is an only child from San Francisco. Perhaps you're an American of Hispanic descent preparing to marry a man or woman who is Caucasian or African-American. Whatever your background, you realize that you and your fiancé or spouse are approaching marriage with different family backgrounds, varying cultural heritages, contrasting ways of communicating, and differing worldviews and values. Congratulations! Recognizing these differences and being proactive about addressing them is the first step to building a healthy, happy, and successful intercultural marriage.

Entering an intercultural marriage requires a gigantic leap of faith. Most likely the excitement of new love and all its emotions are coursing through your veins, filling you with the thrill of anticipation. However, you may also feel stress as you shoulder the burden of the wedding planning, the financial decisions, the paperwork, the traveling, and deciding how to deal with your in-laws—you have so much to do in such a short time!

Truth be told, the average couple spends much more time planning their **wedding** than planning for their **marriage**. Recent studies indicate that the average couple in America spends between two and three hundred hours and around $22,000 planning their wedding ceremony, but only a few hours (if any) in marriage preparation and premarital counseling. Most young couples focus almost exclusively on their wedding while harboring naïve, idealistic, and deeply romantic notions about the future of their marriage.

But intercultural couples represent the exception to the rule. Consider the following surprising statistics regarding intercultural couples in America:

1. They are **more likely** to have an advanced education (such as a master's degree, Ph.D., or M.D.) than non-intercultural couples.

2. They are often **better off financially** than traditional couples.

3. They are often **older** at the age of marriage than traditional couples.

4. They recognize that **they will face cultural obstacles in marriage**, and they want powerful resources to help them overcome those obstacles.

In preparing for marriage, *intercultural couples spend more time and money than traditional couples* searching for practical marriage preparation resources to guide them in the years ahead. Rather than taking a naïve approach to marriage, they recognize that they will likely face more obstacles than the average American couple, and they want to be able to pinpoint and neutralize potential problem areas before they arise. I know this from personal experience, as I once also searched for a book like *Your Intercultural Marriage* to help me discover what to expect from my own intercultural marriage.

Few experiences match the joy, excitement, and mystery of falling in love with a person from another country or culture.

Years ago, a young man from Romania captured my heart as we served together on a mission team in his home country. Our love for each other grew as we laughed and worked together, hosting youth camps for orphans in the breathtakingly beautiful Carpathian Mountains. Catalin's love for God, his integrity, his work ethic, his sense of humor, and his care for the orphan children were so evident. Over time, God clearly revealed that this man was the one for me!

After Catalin asked me to marry him, the excitement of our love and the prospect of this fascinating new adventure enthralled me, but a terrifying reality also stared me in the face: I had just agreed to marry someone from a culture completely different from my own. Was I truly ready to take this enormous leap of faith and marry a man from half a world away? Was I prepared emotionally, spiritually, and physically for the strenuous challenges that lay ahead?

I decided to start doing some research to see what I was getting myself into! Before our wedding, I scoured bookstores and spent hours online, searching for relevant resources. I also contacted friends and family members who had entered intercultural marriages to ask if they had discovered any informative Christian resources. I passionately desired to know what to expect from marriage, how to prepare for what lay ahead, and how to anticipate and overcome intercultural conflicts so that my marriage to Catalin would glorify God and last a lifetime.

What did I find in the way of resources? ***Virtually nothing.***

The few outdated resources that I did locate failed to address many of the specific questions that I had. Most of them did not offer me practical advice on how to build a happy, healthy marriage. Even more disappointing, very few of the available books on intercultural marriage had been written by Christian authors. Most of the resources I found did not present a Christian perspective on the issue of intercultural marriage or offer godly, biblical principles that my fiancé and I could use in building our marriage on a firm foundation.

At that time, I determined that once I had gleaned more experience from my own marriage and had interviewed an extensive cross-section of intercultural couples, I would write the resource that I had desperately searched for but could never find: the definitive guide to intercultural marriage. That's how *Your Intercultural Marriage* came into being.

When I began interviewing couples as part of the research for my book, I received the following responses from virtually every couple:

1. **"We're so glad you're writing this book! We searched for a resource like this before we got married and couldn't find a single one."**

2. **"Please let us know as soon as the book is published so we can buy it. We desperately need it!"**

I wrote this book for all of those couples who have been seeking a resource to help them build strong marriages on the firm foundation of Jesus Christ. I have sought to minister to the needs of millions of intercultural couples by offering them this biblical, practical, life-giving resource.

To help make this a useful, God-centered, Christian resource on the subject of intercultural marriage, I have provided many personal insights on the issue gleaned from my own experiences, including funny and poignant anecdotes drawn from my own marriage. You'll also find biblical principles, powerful examples, and wise advice from the many Christian intercultural couples I have interviewed and asked to contribute.

My fervent desire is that you will find this book a comprehensive, fun to read, and practical resource as you seek to build a God-honoring intercultural marriage. For additional resources on intercultural marriage or to contact me with comments or questions, please visit my Web site at www.marriageleap.com. I'm praying for you as you read this book. My hope is that the principles found here will guide you and provide a strong foundation for your marital journey. May God bless you as you take this exciting leap of faith!

—Marla Alupoaicei

1 [Discovering the Joys and Benefits of Intercultural Marriage]

A SUCCESSFUL marriage requires falling
in love many times, always with the same person.

[Mignon McLaughlin[1]]

M y wedding day had finally arrived. My handsome groom, Catalin, and I stood before the mayor of the city of Falticeni, Romania, while he performed our ceremony. Then we led the wedding procession back to his family's home, where my mother-in-law served a sumptuous wedding feast. Each course could have been an entire meal in itself: silver trays of carefully arranged aperitifs; tender slabs of steak, roast beef, and ham; platters piled high with traditional Romanian meat-and-rice rolls called *salmale*; and my favorite: the lovely, deceptively light, filled pastries. Each selection was a work of art unto itself, almost too pretty to eat.

As the crowning touch, my husband's mother dimmed the lights in the dining room and brought out a seven-layer cake glowing with a ring of lighted candles. On top of the cake, the words *CASA DE PIATRA* were spelled out in flowing script. Not familiar with this Romanian phrase, I asked my husband what it meant. "House like a Rock," he said. "It's the greatest wedding blessing that we could receive."

So simple, yet so profound: House like a Rock. At that moment, God impressed on my heart that a house like a rock can only be a house built on *The Rock*—Jesus Christ. A marriage that lasts will be anchored to the foundation of God's Word. Jesus said, "If you work [My] words into your life, you are like a smart carpenter who built his house on solid rock. Rain poured down, the river flooded, a tornado hit—but nothing moved that house. . . . But if you . . . don't work them into your life, you are like a stupid carpenter who built his house on the sandy beach. When a storm rolled in and the waves came up, it collapsed like a house of cards" (Matthew 7:24–27 THE MESSAGE).

Ever built a lavish sand castle on a beach? For six years during my childhood, I lived in Fort Myers, Florida. I loved building intricate sand castles, complete with moats, drawbridges, and always a special tower for the princess. But no matter how lofty or beautiful the structure, the tide never failed to come in and wash it away. At first, the seawater lapped gently at the foundation. Then the tide began to steal bits of sand. Next, the base of the castle started to sag toward the Gulf. Eventually, the entire structure washed away, leaving behind only the memory of all the time I had invested into building my dream home.

Sadly, I've met many intercultural couples who have built their marriages on sinking sand instead of cementing them to the solid foundation of God's Word. Like a little girl's sand castles, their homes are at risk of toppling and being washed out to sea unless they discover the absolute importance of building their marriages on the Rock of Ages—Jesus Christ.

On the day of our wedding, Catalin and I stood transfixed as we looked into each other's eyes. We felt the same bliss that many couples share on their wedding day; finally, we'd found that perfect person to complete us.

Years later, we're still deeply in love with each other. But we've discovered that intercultural marriage is a lifelong building project. The idealism and naïveté that caused us such euphoria on our wedding day has been replaced by deeper wisdom and a commitment to love each other despite difficult obstacles. We've laughed over misunderstandings—and we've cried over them, too. My desire is to share our experiences and the stories of hundreds of other intercultural couples with you so that you'll be equipped with the blueprint and the tools to build your house on the Rock as well.

Forget about 50/50 . . .
Marriage Is a Covenant

Since Catalin and I married, I've discovered that the world's concept of marriage and God's concept of marriage couldn't be more different. The world says, "Marriage is a 50/50 proposition." God's view of marriage says, "I pledge to give you 100 percent, even if you can't give me anything in return" (Ephesians 5:22–33). The world says, "Marriage is a legal business contract that can be voided if we encounter 'irreconcilable differences.'" God says, "Marriage is a sacred covenant" (Genesis 2:18–25; Matthew 19:3–9). And have you ever noticed that Scripture doesn't mention *anything* about irreconcilable differences?

Intercultural marriage involves a sacred, binding covenant made between God and two people from different cultures, countries, or ethnic groups. And it's a covenant that the Lord wants us to keep—but keeping it isn't easy. For a few years, my husband and I coasted along as smoothly as an Olympic ice-skating pair. But the past few years of our marriage have required us to do some deeper soul-searching. As a result, we've grown in wisdom, faith, maturity, and patience, and we wouldn't trade our rich intercultural partnership for the world.

Intercultural couples may experience more conflict than the average couple. However, they also experience extraordinary benefits as a result of their willingness to take that leap of faith. In my conversations with intercultural couples from all over the globe, I've identified a multitude of blessings that intercultural couples receive as the result of their partnerships. Whether your journey is just beginning or you've been married for fifty years, keep these benefits in mind during the days ahead.

The Joys and Benefits of Intercultural Marriage

Appreciating Other Cultures and Overcoming Stereotypes

Intercultural couples have the opportunity to cultivate a greater appreciation for other cultures. In her book *Intercultural Marriage: Promises & Pitfalls*, Dugan Romano writes, "Because of exposure to different customs, ceremonies, languages, and countries, most couples felt that they had enriched their daily lives in a way which would probably not have been possible with someone from the same background. They often felt that life with a 'foreigner' was more consistently interesting because it was more varied and unpredictable."[2] Catalin and I have grown to appreciate the ways in which our cultures differ. With each new stamp we've received on our passports, we've collected funny stories, valuable experiences, and priceless memories, and our lives have gained greater vitality.

Marrying a person from another culture also provides couples with the impetus to overcome their personal stereotypes. Intercultural marriage (and the experience of interacting with people in different cultures) brings to the surface deeply seated prejudices and assumptions that most people don't even realize that they possess. Here's a funny example of prejudice from early in our marriage. My husband writes certain numbers (such as 1, 4, and 9) differently than most Americans do. Once, when he and I visited the university library, he wrote down our phone number for the librarian. She looked at the number and asked him, "Why do you make your '4s' so funny?"

He replied matter-of-factly, "Why do you make *yours* so funny?" I burst out laughing. He had a point: Who says that the way we Americans write the number 4 is "right"? In fact, neither way is necessarily correct; they're just *different*. But we tend to conclude, "My way is right; yours is wrong." Intercultural couples learn quickly that they must change this way of thinking in order to achieve harmony in their marriages.

When I married Catalin, I learned that the American way of doing things is *a* way of doing things, not necessarily the *right* way. I also learned that God is not American, and neither is Christianity. When we open our minds and hearts to these truths, our relationships with others improve in all areas of our lives.

Gaining a Multicultural Family and Children

Another benefit of intercultural marriage is the blessing of gaining a multicultural family and rearing multicultural

children. While children of intercultural couples may encounter some challenges that typical children don't face, they
also reap rich rewards as a result of their intercultural heritage.
One intercultural couple, Dorrie and Hiroshi, said of their bicultural children: "They grew up with a global worldview and
are just naturally sensitive to the nuances of different cultures;
[we] like to think that the world is in their hands—that the
time for the true multiculturalist has come, and these kids are
born culture-brokers."[3]

Kim, a child born to intercultural parents, categorizes herself as "Australian-Swiss-Vietnamese." She writes: "As a child
of a multicultural family, I have many challenges, opportunities,
and aspirations. I am entitled to a rich, diverse life. Having parents from different cultures has broadened my horizons so that
I see life through many perspectives. I do not see myself any
longer as different, but as unique. My uniqueness allows me to
be a part of the human race without total loss of individuality.
I try to accept, acknowledge, and be three cultures within one
person. Having intercultural parents teaches you a lot about
love, life . . . the universe."[4]

The Stretching of Minds and Challenging of Worldviews

Intercultural marriage offers couples and their children the
chance to have their minds stretched and their worldviews
challenged. Oliver Wendell Holmes once said, "Man's mind,
once stretched by a new idea, never regains its original dimensions."[5] A worldview is like a pair of glasses; it colors how we
see and interpret reality. When we choose to marry a person
from another culture, we learn to take off our own "worldview
glasses" and take a fresh look at the world through our partner's lenses. We begin to understand why that person thinks,
talks, and acts the way he or she does. We also have the opportunity to address the differences between reality and various cultures' *perceptions* of that reality.

More Opportunities for Ministry and International Travel

Intercultural couples also gain greater opportunities to be
involved with missions and other ministries. My husband and

I met while working for an orphan ministry in Romania. We love children, and we know how much God loves them, too. Catalin and I feel a special affinity for the children of the world who have been hurt, abused, and abandoned. God has used our shared experiences in orphan ministry in Romania to forge a powerful bond between us. We are now able to minister to intercultural couples in the States. When we meet people here who have emigrated from Romania, we can connect with them and encourage them in their marriages.

Many intercultural couples gain the opportunity (and have a reason) to travel more often. A number of individuals who choose intercultural marriage in the first place are "international souls" who have grown up in other countries or cultures and already feel comfortable traveling from place to place and adjusting to the customs and mores of different cultures. Since we married, Catalin and I have had the opportunity to travel throughout Europe and tour his homeland of Romania. Because I've always enjoyed traveling and having the chance to learn new languages and discover other cultures, intercultural marriage was a natural fit for me. It may be for you as well!

Intercultural couples also enjoy developing an international identity. Many of them spend time jet-setting from culture to culture. I recently met a young woman named Daniela from the Czech Republic who is dating a Romanian man. Both of them live in Switzerland. They can easily make the transition from speaking Czech to German to French to English to Romanian and then back again. People like Daniela feel comfortable traveling to almost any place or culture because of their natural ability to cross language and cultural barriers.

Expanding Our Horizons and Learning New Languages

As a result of the intercultural partnership that Catalin and I have formed, our personal and spiritual horizons have expanded considerably. We see the vast scope of God's redemptive work in the world as He uses ordinary, fallible people like us to show others His plan of salvation through Christ. Both Catalin and I have grown to understand more of God's power and sovereignty, and we're amazed that He is so intimately concerned with the details of our lives. We've also gained a stronger sense of His profound love for all people, no matter their skin color, language, culture, ethnicity, religious beliefs, or worldview.

Another benefit that intercultural couples reap is the opportunity to learn one or more new languages. Catalin worked as a translator for Buckner Orphan Care International and already spoke excellent English when he arrived in the United States, so he had an advantage. But I have learned some Romanian by reading books and listening to tapes, as well as by spending time talking with Catalin and his family on each trip we take to Romania. My love for my husband's beautiful Latin-based language has provided a powerful motivation for me to continue to learn to speak it.

Affirming Each Other's Identity

Intercultural marriage provides us a forum for affirming each other's identity and saying, "You matter to me and to God." We gain the opportunity to encourage and affirm our spouse's experiences, identity, language, family, and culture. Catalin and I live in constant awe that God could bring together two people from half a world away and bond us so closely in heart, soul, body, and spirit. The Lord has granted us a unique, powerful love story that we enjoy sharing with others.

Greater Reliance on God

Christian intercultural couples also gain the opportunity to develop greater reliance on God, which is necessary for a fruitful, Christ-centered marriage. All marriages experience cycles of ebb and flow. Every marriage partner enjoys the high points—the times when the relationship just seems to click. But we're also called to remain committed through the low points, when conflict, depression, dissatisfaction, and other issues may cause us to question our relationship and our choice of marital partner. It doesn't take long for each partner to discover that—surprise!—his or her mate is not perfect. When that lightbulb flashes on, disillusionment sets in.

But often, a positive spiritual result can emerge from this disillusionment. It can motivate couples to attend church more regularly or become involved in small groups, Bible studies, MOPS (Mothers of Preschoolers) groups, or other ministries. They may feel compelled to pray more, both individually and with their spouses. They might seek marriage counseling or advice from others. They may read marriage books to help improve their relationship.

As intercultural couples face hardships, they begin to understand that no flawed, sinful person can meet all of their needs in this life. *Only God can do that.* In 2 Corinthians 12:9, the apostle Paul wrote, "He has said to me, 'My grace is sufficient for you, for power is perfected in weakness.' Most gladly, therefore, I will rather boast about my weaknesses, so that the power of Christ may dwell in me." Our weaknesses provide us with the opportunity to look to God to meet our deepest needs as He molds us into godlier, more mature spouses.

The "Exotic" Factor

For me, as a hopeless romantic, the most enjoyable aspect of intercultural marriage has been the romance. I call this the "exotic" factor. I loved the mystique of falling head-over-heels for a godly and stunning young man from the mysterious nation of Romania. The intrigue of cross-cultural love made the experience compelling and supercharged with excitement—and different from every other dating relationship I had been in. Discovering more about my husband's background, country, language, family, and experiences fascinated me. To this day, Catalin's stories about life in Romania and the country's rich history continue to captivate me and those we meet. Like an archaeologist unearthing treasures from a long-lost empire, I still enjoy discovering new facets of my husband's personality and culture.

A Stronger Commitment

Many intercultural couples develop a diamond-tough commitment to their marriages because of the hard work required and the adversity they must overcome just to be together. The endless stacks of paperwork, the family conflicts, the wedding planning, the fervent prayers for visas to be approved, the difficulties of long-distance communication, the miles of governmental red tape—these require intercultural couples to fight for their marriage before it even begins. This creates a strong bond among intercultural couples that many other couples don't have the opportunity to forge.

A Sense of Adventure

No doubt about it—intercultural marriage is an adventure! Intercultural couples experience the thrill of knowing what it's like to do something "outside of the box."

I've never considered myself an adventurous person, so I was surprised when one friend commented, "You're so brave to have gone to another country and married Catalin!" I had never thought of it that way. I had simply been available for God to use for His purposes, and He led me to my husband in a way that I never anticipated. By being willing to take this leap of faith, I've seen the Lord build my strength, courage, and character as He has prepared me for a fruitful ministry of writing, speaking, and encouraging others.

When God called Abraham to travel to an unknown land, Abraham didn't say, "Send someone else, God." He said, "I'll go." And the entire world was blessed by his obedience. As a result of our willingness to take the intercultural leap of faith, we may have the opportunity to take the gospel into a culture where it is not often heard.

Identifying with Jesus Christ

As people who have been called to cross boundaries of nation, ethnicity, culture, and language, we have the privilege of identifying with Jesus Christ, who left His Father in heaven to live on earth as the Son of God. Philippians 2:7–8 tells us that Jesus "emptied Himself [of glory], taking the form of a bondservant, and being made in the likeness of men. . . . He humbled Himself by becoming obedient to the point of death, even death on a cross." And Isaiah 53:3 says, "He was despised and forsaken of men, a man of sorrows and acquainted with grief."

When we, our spouses, and our children suffer from the lack of understanding expressed by the world, we get a small glimpse of the suffering that Christ experienced on earth. That helps us to identify with Christ and to develop greater compassion for others who have been mistreated, disenfranchised, and alienated. Ironically, many of the heroes and heroines of the Christian faith experienced intense alienation. In fact, the term *Hebrew* in the Old Testament literally meant "foreigner." The book of Hebrews reminds us: "By faith [Abraham] lived as an alien in the land of promise, as in a foreign land, dwelling in tents with Isaac and Jacob, fellow heirs of the same promise" (Hebrews 11:9).

God has always had a special affinity for outsiders. He often reminded His people to take care of those who were hurt, lonely, poor, and sick. He told them, "Show your love for the alien, for you were aliens in the land of Egypt" (Deuteronomy 10:19).

As we identify with Christ and the fellowship of His sufferings, we recognize that He came to earth, died on the cross, and rose from the dead in order to make a way for people of *all* nations, tribes, tongues, and cultures to be reconciled to a holy God. Paul wrote in Ephesians, "But now in Christ Jesus you who formerly were far off have been brought near by the blood of Christ. For He Himself is our peace, who made both groups into one and broke down the barrier of the dividing wall. . . . So then *you are no longer strangers and aliens, but you are fellow citizens with the saints, and are of God's household*" (Ephesians 2:13–14, 19, emphasis mine).

The blessings (and the struggles) that we face in intercultural marriage provide us with a platform for modeling Christ's sacrificial love to our spouses, families, and friends. By being kind and patient with our spouses and children, hanging on to our sense of humor, lovingly working through problems, actively listening to others' stories, and sharing our life experience with others, we demonstrate how God has "broken down the dividing wall" and made all who call on Him brothers and sisters in Christ.

QUOTES *for reflection*

*The Lord God fashioned into a woman the rib which He had
taken from the man, and brought her to the man.
The man said, "This is now bone of my bones,
And flesh of my flesh; She shall be called Woman,
Because she was taken out of Man."
For this reason a man shall leave his father and his mother,
and be joined to his wife; and they shall become one flesh.*
●Genesis 2:22–24

*Know therefore that the Lord your God, He is God,
the faithful God, who keeps His covenant and His lov-
ingkindness to a thousandth generation with those
who love Him and keep His commandments.*
●Deuteronomy 7:9

MOVIES *to watch*

Maid in Manhattan
starring Jennifer Lopez
and Ralph Fiennes
(2002, Rated PG-13)

Shall We Dance?
starring Richard Gere
and Jennifer Lopez
(2004, Rated PG-13)

2 [Understanding Intercultural Marriage Models and Stages]

A GREAT MARRIAGE is not when the "perfect couple" comes together. It is when an imperfect couple learns to enjoy their differences.

[Dave Meurer[1]]

T he Russian author Leo Tolstoy said, "What counts in making a happy marriage is not so much how compatible you are, but how you deal with incompatibility."[2] In some ways, every marriage is intercultural, since each partnership melds two people of different families, heritages, ages, experiences, educational backgrounds, socioeconomic levels, and religious convictions. In fact, a couple in which the husband is from South Boston and the wife is from San Diego may seem more incompatible than a husband and wife from two different countries.

What leads a person to choose an intercultural relationship? What types of people are most likely to stretch beyond their comfort zones to embrace a mate from another country or culture? Let's explore the answers to these questions below.

Individuals Who Choose Intercultural Marriage

My husband and I live in Texas, but every Christmas, we travel to Indiana to celebrate the season with my family. Sometimes I wish I could package that heartwarming Midwestern Christmas mix: the aroma of hazelnut coffee and homemade cookies; time spent laughing with friends and family around the fire; enjoying romantic walks with my husband on crisp evenings; embarking on a late-night, last-minute shopping jaunt with my three sisters.

I always hope for a white Christmas, too. Few experiences

are more magical to me than when I gaze up on Christmas Eve to see huge snowflakes tumbling down like feathers from an angel's wings.

Just as no two snowflakes bear exactly the same crystalline geometry, people's reasons for choosing intercultural marriage vary widely. However, I've found in my research and interviews with intercultural couples that those who choose intercultural marriage tend to possess similar characteristics. We'll look at the seven most common categories below.

Romantics

Romantics comprise the largest group of intercultural couples. (As I mentioned in the previous chapter, I fit into this category myself.) Romantics are optimistic people who believe the best about others and see the world through rose-colored glasses. Idealistic and free-spirited, romantics have a tendency to maximize the "pros" and minimize the "cons" in a given situation.

Romantics get swept up in the fascination of meeting and falling in love with a person from another culture. While they may recognize that intercultural marriage can lead to some misunderstandings, their idealism leads them to believe that love conquers all and that their own love story will be mostly devoid of conflict. Many Americans fit this category, partly due to the way romantic love and intercultural relationships are portrayed in books, movies, and TV shows.

Esmeralda, a classic romantic, was the well-heeled daughter of a Spanish industrialist who fell in love with a Mexican soccer star during the high-spirited Carnival celebration in Rio de Janeiro. Soon after the couple married, Esmeralda faced disillusionment when she discovered that she had based her decision on unrealistic romantic expectations. She had married her mestizo husband with the idea that she was taking a step back in time, entering a mysterious and exciting "primitive" world.[3] Esmeralda eventually realized that she had fallen in love with an idea—a fairy tale of her own making—rather than with a real person. Her marriage with the soccer star did not last long. She blamed the divorce on "Mexican primitiveness"; he blamed it on "Spanish arrogance."[4]

"Romeo and Juliet" Couples

"Romeo and Juliet" couples are formed when two individuals marry from families, religious backgrounds, or cultures that are diametrically opposed to each other. In many cases, one spouse's family or culture is involved in a direct personal, religious, ethnic, or political conflict with the other spouse's family or culture.

This term stems, of course, from the famous Shakespearean tragedy in which the star-crossed lovers Romeo Montague and Juliet Capulet fell deeply in love with each other despite the fact that their families had locked horns in a bitter feud. The two lovers married in secret and hatched a creative plan that would enable them to remain together, but their plan failed through a series of tragic ironies. These two young people's lives were eventually destroyed by the hatred harbored by their families.

The movie *Hotel Rwanda* portrays the true story of a Romeo and Juliet couple—a man named Paul Rusesabagina (played by Don Cheadle) from the majority Hutu tribe married to a woman named Tatiana from the minority Tutsi tribe. These tribes experienced conflict that escalated into ethnic cleansing on a massive scale. The movie details the severe hardships faced by this Romeo and Juliet couple as they tried to escape the horrifying genocide that occurred in Rwanda in 1994, during which at least 800,000 people were brutally murdered.[5]

Dawn, the daughter of a Jewish doctor, chose to marry a man of German heritage partly as a way of breaking free from some of the limiting expectations put upon her as a "Jewish-American Princess" by her parents. Dawn says that at the time of her marriage she had a rebellious streak, but after several years of marriage, both members of this couple became Christians and are now actively involved in ministry, along with their three children.

Despite the major cultural clashes that Romeo and Juliet couples encounter, some of them are able to reconcile those differences and forge a new identity together. They realize that in order to build a successful marriage, they must distance themselves from the conflicts and prejudices of their families and cultures of origin.

Internationals

Internationals find intercultural marriage to be a natural fit because they've grown up in a culture or country other than their own. Their parents may have served as military service-people, professors, researchers, diplomats, missionaries, ministry leaders, or business executives in other cultures. Some internationals may be the children of intercultural parents themselves, or the children of parents who enjoyed traveling widely.

One international, an American Foreign Service officer, felt that meeting his wife while in training in Taiwan made perfect sense. He was in his late twenties, dating, and ready to find a lifetime partner. He was part of a community in which intercultural marriage seemed perfectly logical, while "going home to settle down" would have been completely at odds with his career plans. Meeting and marrying a woman from Taiwan seemed the natural choice for him.[6]

Rebels

Rebels choose intercultural marriage as a way of going against the crowd, expressing their individuality, or as a means of "getting back" at their parents, relatives, or friends. Jaime, a young man from Santo Domingo, fits this description.

One evening, Jaime sauntered into a restaurant with a group of Latin friends, laughing and talking. He noticed Cassie—a quiet, pretty girl who worked at the restaurant as a waitress. As Jaime began to talk with Cassie, he discovered that her mannerisms, personality, and beliefs stood in sharp contrast to those of his family and his culture—and Jaime was hooked. Soon afterward, the two began dating and eventually married.

Cassie "personified freedom from all the things [Jaime] objected to. She was the embodiment of what he considered 'American.' Not only was she pretty in a natural way and forthright rather than flirty—unlike the girls from his social group in Santo Domingo—but she was free and fun and broke all the rules . . . and she adored him, not a small matter for a lonesome student far from his homeland. Added to that was the spice of knowing that she was someone his parents wouldn't (and didn't) approve of—wrong religion, different social milieu."[7]

As in Jaime's case, many rebels deliberately pick a marriage partner that they know their parents will not approve of. In some cases, those who make this choice do so because they feel that they haven't been unconditionally loved or accepted by their parents or families. As a result, they may (either consciously or subconsciously) attempt to hurt or alienate their families by choosing a spouse that they know will cause division. They may do this as a means of lashing out, or in hopes that the family's focus on the intercultural spouse will deflect negative attention away from themselves.

Other rebels may never have felt accepted by their peers or their culture. Some may oppose the government of their country or feel too restricted by the laws, customs, traditions, or religious mores of their home culture. They may choose to marry a person who represents a departure from these as a way to speak out against certain aspects of their own culture that they don't agree with.

Some rebels marry interculturally simply because they desire the freedom to live in a different culture or country and to make their own decisions without the influence of their parents, family members, or friends.

Other rebels may actually be considered the "golden child" of the family. As a result of the pressure to live up to others' expectations, these rebels choose intercultural marriage as a way of breaking the mold or surprising their families and friends. This is not necessarily a negative decision; however, if the rebel deliberately chooses a spouse that his or her parents don't approve of, severe conflict will likely ensue. Rebels must guard against using their intercultural spouse as a "weapon" for getting back at their parents, families, or cultures.

Compensators

Compensators choose an intercultural spouse to complete them in some significant way. They desire a mate who will compensate for some aspect of their personality, culture, childhood, family life, or other area that they feel is lacking.

Jaime's wife, Cassie, was a classic compensator. When she saw the handsome, exuberant young man from Santo Domingo stroll into the restaurant where she worked, Cassie was drawn to him like a moth to a flame.

Cassie was attracted to Jaime, in part, because she felt like the leftover offspring of her mother's failed first marriage. Her father had abandoned the family when Cassie was twelve, and Cassie's mother quickly remarried and had three children by her second husband. Since then, Cassie had felt like she was in the way in this new family. She felt tall and gawky, and she was also moody, unpopular in her peer group, unhappy at home, and unsuccessful in school.[8] Jaime represented everything that Cassie was not but wanted to be. She admired his confidence and hoped that his carefree demeanor would rub off on her.[9]

Most of us choose a life mate who will complement us by challenging us to grow and mature in our areas of weakness. Compensators, however, may go to the extreme in choosing a person so vastly different from themselves that many conflicts arise. In addition, idealistic compensators tend to believe that they will become much more like their spouses, when, in fact, their personalities typically don't change much.

Nontraditionals

Nontraditionals are people who, for whatever reason, don't feel fully a part of their own culture. My husband, Catalin, feels that this category best fits him. He became a Christian soon after the fall of the Berlin Wall in Germany and the revolution in Romania in 1989, during which the oppressive dictator Nicolae Ceaușescu and his wife, Elena, were deposed.

As evangelical Christians, Catalin and his family became a small minority in a nation in which most people follow the Orthodox religion. Like Judaism, the Orthodox religion possesses strong cultural and traditional elements. Those who chose to embrace a different faith are considered traitors not only to the Orthodox religion, but in a sense, to the Romanian culture.

But Catalin grew strong in his faith as a result of being in the minority. A brilliant thinker with a curious mind, he excelled at math and science as well as in literature and languages.

He never fit the "status quo" of Romanian teenagers; he was more progressive and open-minded. In his early teens, he began working as a translator for American and British mission teams traveling to Romania.

From a young age, he focused on learning English as well as possible because he felt certain that he would live in an English-speaking country at some point. Because of his willingness to embrace other cultures so openly, intercultural marriage was a more natural fit for him than marrying a person from his own culture, and that has been a blessing for me.

Missions-Minded Individuals

Some people choose a spouse from another country or culture because they feel led to be involved with missions or another ministry in that culture. Our friends Jason (American) and Liliam (Brazilian) moved to Brazil after graduating from seminary. They live closer to Liliam's family now, and they also serve as missionaries, training and mobilizing Brazilians to be sent out as missionaries to other cultures.

Four Intercultural Marriage Models

Most intercultural marriages fit one of four models. The first is *consensus*.[10]

CONSENSUS

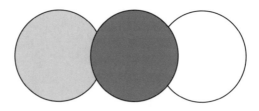

In this system, couples agree on which aspects of their beliefs, values, worldviews, traditions, languages, and cultures will be integrated into the marriage and daily life. These couples are able to include many aspects of their individual cultures in their marriages without losing their identity together. Our friends Gil (Puerto Rican) and Elena (Macedonian) fit this model. They live in the States and do an excellent job of maintaining their ties to their families and cultures while also creating a positive marriage partnership with its own dynamics.

The second model is *compromise.*[11]

COMPROMISE

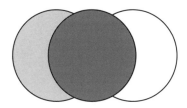

In this model, each individual gives up a substantial amount of his or her culture, language, and traditions in order to keep the peace. Many of each person's individual personality characteristics, preferences, habits, traditions, and cultural ties are sacrificed in order to create harmony in the relationship. This may be the case for individuals whose cultures clash more than usual in terms of male and female roles, ideas about child rearing, religious views, and so on. It also applies often to couples who have chosen to live in a third country or culture where each spouse has to make cultural compromises.

The third model is *immersion.*[12]

IMMERSION

In this model, one partner completely (or almost completely) immerses himself or herself in the culture of the other. Catalin and I follow this model, since he has immersed himself in American culture. This model can work well as long as the immersed partner has willingly chosen to do so. Catalin has enjoyed being a part of American culture and has never seemed resentful of it. On the other hand, I enjoy his cultural heritage and encourage him to keep in contact with his family and friends. We visit his family in Romania as often as possible. Catalin has never pressured or expected me to speak his language perfectly, eat (or cook) Romanian food in our home, dress, or act the way that women in his culture do. Some men and women may face pressure from their spouses to do these things, which can cause conflict.

The fourth model is *eclipse* (also called *obliteration*).[13]

ECLIPSE

In this model, the distinct language, culture, and identity of both partners are eclipsed by that of a third, shared identity. Both partners give up virtually all of their own customs and heritage to adopt that of a third culture. Many "Romeo and Juliet" couples end up following the eclipse model in order to keep the peace. Couples who adopt the eclipse model choose to move to neutral ground, which enables them to break free from the familial, cultural, religious, and governmental restrictions of their own cultures.

The Four Stages of Marriage

The development of a good marriage is not a natural process. It is an achievement.

—David and Vera Mace[14]

Just as a person journeys through the stages of childhood, adolescence, and adulthood, every marriage passes through seasons of fruitfulness and seasons of dryness.

In his book *The Four Seasons of Marriage*, Gary Chapman writes:

> My experience, both in my own marriage and in counseling couples for more than thirty years, suggests that marriages are perpetually in a state of transition, continually moving from one season to another. . . . Sometimes we find ourselves in winter . . . other times we experience springtime, with its openness, hope, and anticipation. On still other occasions we bask in the warmth of summer—comfortable, relaxed, enjoying life. And then comes fall with its uncertainty, negligence, and apprehension. The cycle repeats itself many times throughout the life of a marriage, just as the seasons repeat themselves in nature.[15]

Think about the stage your own relationship may be in as you read the descriptions of each season below.

Spring

Marriages begin in the honeymoon period of spring, with the soaring emotions that accompany the experience of falling head-over-heels in love with a person from another culture. One newlywed describes her marriage this way: "It's full of joy! It's exciting to watch our relationship grow and develop. That 'in love' high just deepens and becomes richer each day. Every day is an opportunity to find a way to live out my love for my husband."[16]

Summer

The summer season of marriage manifests a deepening of love, a strengthening of a couple's connection to each other. The initial honeymoon effects of spring may have waned, but summer marriages reflect a sense of security, commitment, and satisfaction. Julia, married for sixteen years, says: "Summer feels good. We're on the same page, and that makes our marriage fun. It opens up my heart to communication."[17]

Fall

Fall is the prelude to winter. Couples in the fall season recognize that the winds of change are blowing and that their relationship is facing trouble. A man who has been married for thirty-one years said, "I feel dejected, disheartened, and unappreciated. It's not a good place to be. I am not content with my marriage. Something has got to change or we're not going to make it."[18]

Winter

The winter season of marriage is characterized by stormy weather: emotions of hurt, anger, disappointment, loneliness, grief, and rejection. Dr. Chapman writes, "What brings a couple to the winter season of marriage? In a word: *rigidity*—the unwillingness to consider the other person's perspective and to work toward a meaningful compromise."[19]

What's a couple in the winter season to do? These seven strategies, outlined in greater detail in the book *The Four Seasons of Marriage*, will enable a struggling intercultural couple to move through winter toward spring.

1. Deal with past failures.

2. Choose a winning attitude.

3. Learn to speak your spouse's love language.
   (For more information, see Dr. Gary Chapman's excellent book *The Five Love Languages* [Northfield Publishing, 1995].)

4. Develop the awesome power of empathetic listening.

5. Discover the joy of helping your spouse succeed.

6. Maximize your differences.

7. Implement the power of positive influence.[20]

Every marriage will pass through these seasons, but thankfully, winter doesn't last forever. Spring is right around the corner! My prayer is that understanding the implications of these intercultural marriage models and patterns will help you improve your communication as a couple. Practicing these principles will empower you and your spouse to create deeper bonds of love and unity as an intercultural couple.

QUOTE *for reflection*

Wives, be subject to your own husbands, as to the Lord. . . .
as the church is subject to Christ, so also the wives ought
to be to their husbands in everything.
Husbands, love your wives, just as Christ also loved the
church and gave Himself up for her. . . . So husbands ought
also to love their own wives as their own bodies. He who
loves his own wife loves himself; for no one ever hated his
own flesh, but nourishes and cherishes it, just as Christ also
does the church, because we are members of His body.
●Ephesians 5:22, 24–25, 28–30

MOVIES *to watch*

Fools Rush In
starring Matthew Perry
and Salma Hayek
(1997, Rated PG-13)

French Kiss
starring Meg Ryan
and Kevin Kline
(1995, Rated PG-13)

Hotel Rwanda
starring Don Cheadle
and Sophie Okonedo
(2004, rated PG-13)

3 [Surviving (and Enjoying) Your Engagement, Wedding, and Honeymoon]

MAYBE HONEYMOONS are God's anesthesia. Like the "laughing gas" used by dentists, perhaps honeymoons are designed to protect us from a bit of the pain and fear involved in doing something that, while scary and uncomfortable, is for our own good in the long run.

[SUE PATTON THOELE[1]]

So you've fallen in love with a man or a woman from another culture. Congratulations! But what's next? How can you wisely navigate the waters of dating, engagement, and planning a wedding ceremony and a honeymoon—especially if you and your beloved live in different countries?

The Dating and Engagement Period

Take a Year to Date

If possible, spend at least a year dating before your engagement. If you live apart, spend that time writing letters, talking on the phone, e-mailing, and otherwise communicating as much as possible before getting married. Ed Young, the pastor of Fellowship Church in Grapevine, Texas, suggests, "When you find the person you think is 'the one,' give yourself a year to observe how that person passes through all of the seasons." Not only will you see how that person acts during each season of the year, but also how that person responds to changes in the seasons of life (conflicts with friends or family, illness, the loss of a job, a move, financial ups and downs, and so on).

Dating for a year will offer you a cooling-off period, and it also will grant you the opportunity to discuss issues and work through conflicts over a significant length of time. You'll see how your beloved handles joys and setbacks, and his or her true colors will be more likely to show. The Bible says that a godly person will

> not walk in the counsel of the wicked. . . .
> But his delight is in the law of the Lord,
> And in His law he meditates day and night.
> He will be like a tree firmly planted by streams of water,
> Which yields its fruit in its season. (Psalm 1:1–3)

Does this describe the man or woman you plan to marry? If not, or if you see other red flags that indicate possible problem areas in your relationship, be sure to consult a trusted pastor or Christian counselor before tying the knot.

How much can a person change in the course of a year? Consider the example of Lynn and Hans. Hans was a dashing young Austrian who worked as a ski instructor at the posh ski resort of St. Anton, Austria. One winter, Lynn (an American) trekked to St. Anton and ended up as a student in one of Hans's ski classes. Beautiful, wealthy, well-educated, and used to living a privileged lifestyle, Lynn immediately felt attracted to Hans and intrigued by his radically different upbringing. He, in turn, was fascinated by this cultured American woman. When Lynn began dating Hans, he reveled in the prestige. They married soon afterward. Hans started wearing a cowboy hat on the slopes to show his "American pride."

Lynn and Hans described the early days of marriage in their winter paradise as being like "a giant slalom" into which they put all their energy. But they were living in vacationland. They didn't open up to one another about their pasts or their insecurities. They didn't discuss how they envisioned their future together. They just lived for the moment.

Then something radical happened—the ski season ended, and the "rain and mud season" began. Suddenly, the honeymoon was over. The nearby hotels and restaurants closed down, and all of the tourists went home. The walls of the couple's tiny apartment began to close in on Lynn; she started to feel lonely, depressed, and discontent. But Hans had immediately transitioned into his off-season routine, leaving Lynn alone at the apartment while he hung out for hours at the corner bar, drinking beer and reminiscing with his fellow ski instructors.

Lynn didn't have a single girlfriend to talk to, and no family members to go places with. She struggled with the "outsider blues" and began to wonder if she had made the right choice in marrying Hans.[2]

Don't be caught off guard like Lynn was; take the effort to see your beloved transition through the seasons. You may be in for a big surprise.

Ask Yourself Serious Questions

During the year that you and your significant other spend dating, ask some serious questions about your relationship. One man who married a woman from Japan recommends asking yourself:

> Is this someone you would [date or marry] even if you were safe and happy in your own country? . . . Culture shock can do funny things to a normally rational mind. Sure, you're lonely; sure, there are things about your surroundings that you just can't seem to figure out; sure, your partner makes everything seem safe by filling you in on the subtle nuances of his or her culture. That's the formula for a perfect couple, right? Wrong. What you have is a parent or a teacher, not a lover. And it's all too easy to overlook [that aspect] when it seems so obvious that this is the 'perfect' person for you.[3]

He continues, "If you see this happening to you, stop. Postpone any commitment. Get yourself comfortable with your surroundings. Disarm the 'convenience' in the relationship, and then see what you think. Learn more about the subtle parts of your partner's culture and then decide if you can tolerate, work with, and actually love that person *because* they are different and not *despite* those differences."[4]

Before you marry, I recommend reading *Finding the Love*

of Your Life: Ten Principles for Choosing the Right Marriage Partner by Neil Clark Warren. Also, every intercultural couple should attend at least three to six months of premarital counseling with a licensed Christian counselor. If you can find a counselor who specializes in helping intercultural couples, even better! If your fiancé lives in another country, each of you should attend counseling separately and then discuss what you have learned. Ask your counselor for a list of important questions to ask your fiancé before marriage. These two books also provide excellent questions that you and your partner can ask each other in the premarital stage:

- *101 Questions to Ask Before You Get Engaged* by H. Norman Wright and Gary J. Oliver

- *1001 Questions to Ask Before You Get Married* by Monica Mendez Leahy

Consider Your Level of Interest in the Other Person's Culture

Intercultural couples usually meet in one or the other's home country. Catalin and I met in Romania (his home country). Our mission team flew into Budapest, Hungary, and then rode a train from Budapest into Romania. Taking that train ride through Eastern Europe for the first time was a powerful experience for me. We passed dazzling fields of bright sunflowers and saw men driving wooden horse-drawn carts down country roads. I felt like I had fallen through Alice in Wonderland's rabbit hole and time-traveled back a hundred years. During my two weeks in Romania, I experienced a deep affinity for the wild, beautiful landscape and the people and language of Romania. In a sense, being there felt like coming home.

Don't underestimate the importance of liking your partner's culture. This means not just appreciating it on a superficial level; do you actually *enjoy* being a part of it? Are you interested enough in it to spend the rest of your life studying the people, history, and language?

Also, ponder the following question: *If the two of you as a couple had to live in either partner's culture indefinitely, could you do it?*

Once you are married, a job change or loss, an illness, a death in the family, financial hardship, religious persecution, a war, a medical issue, or another need could surface that would suddenly require that you move to your spouse's culture, or vice versa. And it's possible that you would have to stay there long term—and perhaps permanently.

"Don't think you can plan to marry someone of another culture if you're not interested in that culture," says Linda Reinisch, who married cross-culturally.[5] Before getting engaged, be sure to discuss your expectations (and your spouse's) about where you will live, how often you will visit your partner's family and culture, and what you will do in case of a family emergency.

Communicate

Open communication during this period of time is crucial; it sets the stage for your communication patterns later in marriage. As you plan your wedding and begin to interact more closely with each other's families, you'll find that your family members and friends (or those of your fiancé) may not understand your decision to marry a person from another culture. You may be shocked to receive the following responses:

- Being asked if that person is planning to marry you only to get a visa to enter your country (or to stay in or travel to a particular country)
- Rejection of you and/or your chosen spouse
- Being completely disowned by your or your future spouse's parents or family
- Refusal to attend the wedding or support the marriage
- Others trying to talk you or your future spouse out of marriage

- Prejudice by family members, friends, and even strangers

- The refusal to accept one or both partners' children into the family

Dealing with these unexpected reactions can be extremely painful for intercultural couples. Do your best to remain gracious with those who express concern. If concern is expressed by people whose wisdom you truly value, consider what they have shared with you. If not, simply don't take the bait.

Having to overcome early opposition will help you and your partner forge a stronger bond. Strive to keep communication lines open at all times. If necessary, choose an object and make a rule that whomever holds that object has the "floor" to speak. Partners can take turns holding the object and speaking their mind on whatever issue is being discussed.

If you and your loved one are separated during your engagement period, never underestimate the power of the traditional, handwritten love letter in our high-tech society. I have a cedar chest that holds the special handwritten love letters, cards, and gifts Catalin has given me. These tokens of his affection are some of my most prized possessions.

You'll enjoy having a tangible record of your relationship. And these cards and letters serve a practical purpose, as well; in your immigration interviews, you will need to provide proof of your relationship. A large sheaf of love letters goes a long way!

If you talk with your beloved mainly by phone, you can save hundreds of dollars by purchasing calling cards at www.callingcards.com. Before my husband and I started using these, I paid *$3 a minute* to call Romania. But by purchasing a simple $20 calling card online, I could talk to him for 206 minutes. Big difference! This site includes affordable cards that will enable you to call almost any country in the world. You can also purchase cards that work specifically for cell phones.

If you and your significant other have access to computers, sign up for Skype (http://skype.com), a service that allows you to talk for free via the Internet with other Skype users. You can also speak with people on landline phones or cell phones, even if they don't have Skype, for a minimal fee.

Another excellent option is Yahoo Messenger, a service that enables you to communicate for free in real time via the Internet. To download this free service, see http://messenger.yahoo.com.

Do Your Research

When the butterflies of bliss make you want to throw all caution to the wind, remember that wise planning is vital to building a solid marriage in Christ. Before you marry, read these two books together and then discuss them as a couple:

- *Before You Say "I Do"* by H. Norman Wright and Wes Roberts (an excellent marriage preparation workbook that Catalin and I used before we married)

- *Saving Your Marriage Before It Starts* by Les and Leslie Parrott

The Wedding

If you've attended an American wedding lately, you realize the jaw-dropping amount of work, time, planning, expense, and attention to detail required to plan a nuptial ceremony. As we have already seen, the typical couple spends much more time planning their wedding than they do their marriage.

Fortunately, you've taken an excellent step toward planning your intercultural marriage—you have purchased this book. Next, set aside some time to get organized. An hour or two of pre-planning will save you countless hours and headaches later. As soon as possible, purchase a large accordion file (or set aside a certain portion of your filing cabinet) for storing your immigration paperwork and other important documents.

In the United States, the official Web site for obtaining information about immigration, visas, citizenship, and more is the U.S. Citizenship and Immigration Services site (www.uscis.gov). This official site includes free downloadable forms for your use. Other sites may also offer these forms, but they charge a fee, and they may not have the most recent version of the forms. Using an older form could result in your application being denied, so be sure to use the www.uscis.gov site. If you are an American citizen living abroad, look up the U.S. embassy in your area and contact it for information.

When you *submit* your official immigration application to the USCIS, you will be required to include a payment to the U.S. government, usually in the form of a personal check or cashier's check.

Your or your fiancé's immigration process may vary significantly depending on a variety of factors, including:

- Country of origin
- Country of planned emigration
- Political and religious factors in the country of origin and country of emigration
- Date of planned emigration
- What type of visa the immigrant currently has, if any (work visa, student visa, etc.)
- What type of visa the immigrant is applying for (marriage immigration visa, fiancé(e) visa, work visa, student visa, seeking political asylum, etc.)
- The circumstances of your marriage

In most cases, you and your spouse will be required to appear in person for an immigration interview. For a list of immigration interview do's and don'ts, see the FindLaw Web site at http://immigration.findlaw.com/immigration/immigration-overview/immigration-overview-interview.html.

Catalin was living in Romania and I was living in the States when we got engaged. We investigated the immigration process and options. We also interviewed intercultural friends who had gone through both the marriage immigration visa process and the fiancé immigration visa process. Catalin discovered that if we applied for the fiancé visa, the process could take up to two years. However, if we married in Romania, he would be able to receive a visa almost immediately as the spouse of an American citizen. So that's what we did. We got engaged in November 2001, married in a civil ceremony in Romania in March 2002, and on April 12, 2002, he arrived in the States. Nine days later, he received his green card and immediately began working. That summer, he began attending college. We feel strongly that the miraculous speed at which this process happened was a result of God's grace and the hundreds of faithful family members and friends who prayed fervently for us.

However (and this is important) the process has changed since then, and receiving a visa and green card typically takes longer. One of our most precious Romanian friends, Madalina, and her husband, Emanuel (who lives in California), married in Romania in August 2007, but Madalina didn't receive her visa until July 2008. As of this writing, she is in California, but is still waiting for her green card to arrive so she can work.

If you need to send money to your fiancé in another country, the best system I've found is Wal-Mart's MoneyGram international money transfer service. Sending an international money transfer via MoneyGram costs only $9.46 at the time of this writing. Simply take the correct amount of cash with you (the amount you want to send plus $10) and visit the Customer Service desk at your local Wal-Mart store.

Planning the Wedding

You'll be wearing a white gown. Your bridesmaids will be decked out in satin . . . you'll hear *Canon in D* playing as you stroll down the white carpet, holding your father's arm. Your handsome groom will stand at the altar, tears of adoration in his eyes . . .

Or maybe you'll be drinking nine cups of sake and changing into a red kimono after your traditional Japanese ceremony, or taking your vows while standing on a beach in some exotic tropical locale.

Wedding celebrations vary widely across the world. What matters is that finally, your wedding dreams are coming true! Planning your wedding should be one of the best experiences of your life. Even if you're on a tight budget, you'll want to host a special ceremony that reflects your and your fiancé's tastes, cultures, and values.

When Catalin and I held our church wedding in Indiana, we included a flag ceremony during which the flags of America and Romania were presented while our respective national anthems played. This offered us a memorable way to celebrate the union of our two cultures. In addition, because Catalin's family could not travel to the States to attend the wedding, we asked a special couple in our church, Dom and Beth, to be Catalin's "parents" during the ceremony.

One of my favorite wedding planning guides was *The Everything Wedding Guide* by Janet Anastasio, Michelle Bevilacqua, and Stephanie Peters. Another helpful guide is *The Everything Wedding Organizer* by Shelly Hagen. Here are some other resources that provide excellent wedding advice and tips for integrating cultural customs into your wedding ceremony:

- *A Simple Wedding* by Sharon Hanby-Robie (Christian book)

- *The Christian Wedding Planner* by Jessica North and H. Norman Wright (Christian book)

- *The Knot Ultimate Wedding Planner: Worksheets, Checklists, Etiquette, Calendars, and Answers to Frequently Asked Questions* by Carley Roney

- *The Knot Guide to Wedding Vows and Traditions: Readings, Rituals, Music, Dances, and Toasts* by Carley Roney and editors of The Knot

- *Simple Stunning Wedding Etiquette: Traditions, Answers, and Advice from One of Today's Top Wedding Planners* by Karen Bussen

- *Timeless Traditions: A Couple's Guide to Wedding Customs around the World* by Lisl M. Spangenberg

Many Web sites also offer fantastic wedding planning information, forms, and vendor contacts—absolutely free. Try the following:

- The Knot, www.theknot.com
- My Wedding.com, www.mywedding.com
- Top Wedding Planning Ideas, www.topweddingplan ningideas.com
- WeddingChannel, www.weddingchannel.com

Planning the Honeymoon

When a man takes a new wife, he shall not go out with the army nor be charged with any duty; he shall be free at home one year and shall give happiness to his wife whom he has taken. (Deuteronomy 24:5)

Taking a honeymoon was part of God's plan! Be sure to plan at least a simple honeymoon or weekend getaway for just the two of you after your wedding. If budget is not a factor, consider an elegant honeymoon cruise or a week or two at an all-inclusive resort like Sandals (www.sandals.com). The online Honeymooner's Review Guide (www.honeymoonersreviewguide.com) provides a comprehensive list of honeymoon options, as well. If you need to save money, enjoy a beautiful beachfront honeymoon by focusing on these less-expensive destinations: Florida, Mexico, Thailand, Jamaica, or the Dominican Republic.

The following books provide excellent, detailed information on planning your perfect honeymoon:

- *The Honeymoon of Your Dreams* by Walt Larimore and Susan Crockett

- *101 Top Honeymoon Destinations: The Guide to Perfect Places for Passion* by Elizabeth Arrighi Borsting and Kerren Barbas Steckler

After the Wedding

After you marry, purchase several of the following books to read together as a couple. Catalin and I enjoyed *Love & Respect* by Emerson Eggerichs and *The Five Love Languages* by Gary Chapman. Here are our other recommendations:

- *Becoming Soul Mates* by Les and Leslie Parrott

- *Boundaries in Marriage* by Henry Cloud

- *For Women Only: What You Need to Know about the Inner Lives of Men* by Shaunti Feldhahn

- *For Men Only: A Straightforward Guide to the Inner Lives of Women* by Shaunti and Jeff Feldhahn

- *His Needs, Her Needs: Building an Affair-Proof Marriage* by Willard F. Harley Jr.

- *I Married You, Not Your Family and Nine Other Relationship Myths That Will Ruin Your Marriage* by Linda Mintle

- *The Mystery of Marriage: Meditations on the Miracle* by Mike Mason

- *Sacred Marriage* by Gary L. Thomas

If you have additional questions, concerns, or need more help in the visa, immigration, wedding planning, or honeymoon planning stages, please e-mail me at marla_alupoaicei@yahoo.com. I pray God's blessings on you and your fiancé as you take the intercultural leap together.

QUOTES *for reflection*

I am my beloved's and my beloved is mine.
● Song of Solomon 6:3

Let your speech always be with grace, as though seasoned with salt, so that you will know how you should respond to each person.
● Colossians 4:6

MOVIES *to watch*

Dances with Wolves
starring Mary McDonnell
and Kevin Costner
(1990, Rated PG-13)

My Big Fat Greek Wedding
starring Nia Vardalos
and John Corbett
(2002, Rated PG)

4 [Building Strong Verbal and Nonverbal Communication Skills]

THE GREATEST PROBLEM in communication is the illusion
that it has been accomplished.

[GEORGE BERNARD SHAW[i]]

Catalin and I were driving on the interstate when we saw a sign advertising a new subdivision of homes from a particular builder. He laughed when he saw the name of the company: NuHomes. Obviously, the company's point was to communicate "new homes," but in Romanian, "nu" means "no." Catalin told me, "No Romanian would ever want to buy a home from a builder named 'No Homes'!"

Mexican-American author Art Lucero describes a similar communication gaffe that he made when he first met the family of his Japanese fiancée, Debbie. He writes:

As we got out of the car, I could hear the ferocious barking of a dog. Debbie was excited to introduce me to [her relatives] and was not thinking about the dog. She said, "Oh, good. Koko is here." Being the dog lover that I am, and because my parents owned a pet dog named Cocoa, I immediately assumed that Debbie was referring to the barking dog. . . . In an attempt to make peace with the protective spaniel, I bent down and placed the back of my hand up against the screen door so he could smell my scent. In a soothing voice I said, "It's OK, Cocoa. It's OK, Cocoa." At that moment, as Grandma unlocked the screen door, she said in her broken English, "Nooo . . . dog Sumi . . . me Koko." I wanted to crawl in a hole.[2]

The renowned Italian filmmaker Federico Fellini said, "A different language is a different vision of life."[3] Misinterpretations of words, connotations, and nonverbal cues can cause major communication challenges for intercultural couples. Such mishaps are often compounded by worldview clashes, false assumptions, stereotypes, and other misunderstandings. Often, we don't even question our assumptions until we are shocked to discover that we were completely incorrect—sometimes embarrassingly so.

One author offers this communication advice to intercultural couples:

> Remember that you both will be setting out on an adventure—a full-time first-hand learning experience in the other person's cultural labyrinth. None of us, I am convinced, ever really appreciates how many things we learn about life when we are young that we take for granted every day. We consider many of these things just plain 'common sense,' but they're only common if you and your partner have common backgrounds. Expect the unexpected. Then you won't be disappointed.[4]

Let's explore some pointers that will be useful for intercultural couples in creating and maintaining positive communication.

Helpful Tips for Improving Communication

Learn Each Other's Languages

Intercultural couples tend to experience less stress in marriages in which both partners speak a common language well. Even if both partners do speak one language well, each spouse should also seek to learn the other's native language. The couple's communication will also improve significantly if each person seeks to understand the other's cultural ways and worldviews as they learn the language.

One of the simplest ways to become more proficient in your

spouse's language is to order foreign language DVDs, CDs, tapes, audiobooks, or language books. Check out the following helpful resources (most of which you can find in bookstores or at online retailers like Amazon.com):

- The "Learn in Your Car" Series—This practical series includes CD audiobooks and listening guides in multiple languages.

- The Berlitz "Think and Talk" Series—An excellent learning tool available in multiple languages.

- Topics Entertainment Instant Immersion Courses— Each of these courses includes software for learning a variety of languages.

- Pimsleur Language Programs—These excellent language resources include the "Quick and Simple" series and the "Conversational" series in multiple languages.

- Teach Me! (www.linguashop.com)—This site includes several lines of excellent and affordable language products, including the Teach Me! Series, the On the Road! Series, the Speak! Series, audiobooks for only $12, and more. Available in over forty languages, including Bavarian, Breton, Cornish, and Romansh.

- Rosetta Stone (www.rosettastone.com)—A helpful language series that includes courses in thirty different languages, from Arabic to Welsh.

- Transparent Language (www.transparent.com)—This practical Web site contains free downloadable language software as well as affordable products for learning many different languages. The site also includes useful phrases, games, cultural information, articles, quizzes, and proficiency tests.

- UBI Soft Software—This interactive software is perfect for helping kids and adults learn new languages. These courses (named "My Spanish Coach,"

"My French Coach," etc.) were created for use on Nintendo DS game systems.

In addition to these resources, intercultural couples may consider taking foreign language courses at a local university or community college. Many community colleges offer inexpensive language courses as part of their curriculum or their continuing education programs. Another option is to hire a personal language tutor to teach at-home courses in vocabulary, grammar, and/or conversational speaking.

Learn about Each Other's Cultures

My American friend Mike, who is married to a German woman, once told me, "Be sure to learn your spouse's culture as you learn the language." Because he speaks German well, Mike's family and friends expected him to also understand the ins and outs of the German culture while he was visiting his wife's family in Germany. He explained that he had to learn some things the hard way. For example, he did not realize that Germans have a custom of personally greeting and shaking hands with every person when they enter or leave a room. Saying a casual, corporate "Hi" and "Bye" to the group (which would be fine in America) is considered extremely rude in Germany.

Intercultural couples should seek to assimilate into each other's cultures while they learn the language so that they will be equipped to interact fully in each other's worlds.

Learn Each Other's Love Languages

In his book *The Five Love Languages*, author Gary Chapman has proposed that most people possess one or more of the following love languages:

- Words of affirmation
- Receiving gifts
- Quality time
- Acts of service
- Physical touch[5]

A person's primary love language is the one that most **communicates love to him or her**. Often, a person will use the love language that speaks most to **him or her** and use it as the primary means of showing love to his or her **spouse**. Usually, however, spouses have different primary love languages. For example, the wife's primary love language may be quality time or gifts, while the husband's primary love language may be acts of service or physical touch.

Other love languages (and subcategories of love languages) may come into play in intercultural marriages, as well. For example, cooking excellent meals for one's spouse could be considered a love language of its own in many cultures. In addition, physical touch has at least three components, each of which could be considered its own love language, especially in certain cultures: nonsexual touch (such as that shared by friends holding hands, parents hugging their children, and so on); affectionate touch between spouses (holding hands, hugging, kissing, and cuddling); and sexual intimacy between spouses.

I highly recommend that intercultural couples read *The Five Love Languages* and take the survey to determine their own and their spouse's primary love languages. This can help prevent communication problems. For instance, giving and receiving gifts is one of my primary love languages, but it is not my husband's primary language. Of course, this has led to disappointment at some junctures in my life, but once I realized that the language of gifts just does not connect with Catalin, I was able to focus more on other love languages and come to terms with the fact that he will most likely never be as "gifty" as I am. When he does give me a special gift (like the beautiful classical guitar he gave me for my birthday this year), I celebrate and treasure that gift even more because I realize that he took extra effort to choose it.

Learn to Listen Well

One of my favorite authors, Ernest Hemingway, recommended, "When people talk, listen completely. Most people never listen."[6] Communication is a two-way street. Listening and interpreting comprise just as much a part of the communication experience as speaking does. Yet listening has become a lost art, especially in our "me-first" American culture.

It's been said that "a gossip is one who talks to you about others; a bore is one who talks to you about himself, and a brilliant conversationalist is one who talks to you about yourself."[7] Catalin and I have a friend, Scott, who used to be the owner of my husband's company. Scott is one of the most gifted listeners I've ever met. He's extremely attentive, focusing on every single word that others say in conversation. He makes each person in the room feel like the *only* person in the room. It's amazing how impressed people can be by the "brilliant conversational skills" of a great listener!

Chinese author Man Keung Ho uses the following illustration to describe the importance of listening in the communication process.

The Chinese word *ting* ("listen") is a pictorial composite of five smaller symbols, which represent: (1) the ear, (2) the mind, (3) the eye, (4) the character meaning "one" or "unity," and (5) the heart. This word beautifully illustrates that good listening involves more than sound entering the ear of the listener; *by engaging in active listening, a couple becomes one in heart and spirit.*[8] By listening not only with the ears but with the heart and the soul, intercultural couples can overcome barriers and become better communicators.

Forgive Each Other

Forgiveness is also a crucial aspect of the communication and listening process. It's a simple fact that most intercultural couples will face more misunderstandings than a "typical" couple. Forgiveness and grace help to smooth out these misunderstandings. At times, my husband will say something that I could take offense at, but I realize he doesn't mean it the way it sounded, so I let it go. And he does the same for me.

Others say, "Choose your battles." But you can "lose your battles" (in the sense of stopping them before they start) simply by refusing to argue about petty matters or insignificant misunderstandings. The Bible says,

A gentle answer turns away wrath,
But a harsh word stirs up anger. (Proverbs 15:1)

When an issue is important enough to warrant serious discussion, determine whether or not you and your spouse are at the point where you can discuss it without getting carried away with anger or other emotions. If not, take a rain check or call a "time out" and wait to discuss the issue until both of you cool down.

Intercultural couples also must learn to fight fair. Name-calling and personal attacks should be out of the question at all times. Seek to keep the real issue the real issue and be careful not to say anything that will cause irreparable damage. If you do, you'll regret it later! Hurtful words and actions are very difficult to forget. They cause lingering pain in a marriage relationship.

Early in our marriage, I created what I call the "AND" principle. I determined that I would do my best never to use the following accusations or attacks in conversations with my husband:

- ALWAYS (You *always* do this . . . or You *always* say that.)

- NEVER (You *never* do this . . . or You *never* do that . . . or You *never* say that.)

- DIVORCE (As in, I want a *divorce* . . . or Maybe I should just leave . . . or Maybe you should just leave.)

Protecting our marriage in this way has been a wise choice. I feel that it has enabled us to live in a loving, respectful way with each other and to avoid saying anything that we would regret later.

Be Careful with Nonverbal Communication and Gestures

Nonverbal communication and gestures possess different meanings in different cultures. In America, a smile may mean "yes"; in Asian cultures, it may mean "no." In Albania and Bulgaria, people shake their heads from side to side to mean "yes" and nod their heads up and down to mean "no," which is the opposite of how people in most cultures express these terms.

In some cultures, simple gestures such as pointing to a person or object; giving someone a "thumbs-up" sign; touching a person with the left hand; putting one's hands into one's pockets while speaking to someone; or writing a person's name in red ink can be extremely offensive. For more fascinating information on gestures specific to your spouse's culture, see the book *Multicultural Manners: Essential Rules of Etiquette for the 21ˢᵗ Century* by Norine Dresser.

Guard Your Verbal Communication

In her book *Love and Limerence: The Experience of Being in Love*, Dorothy Tennov presents groundbreaking research into the experience and the feelings of being in love. According to her studies, the feeling of being in love, for most couples, lasts between two and six years.[9] After this period of infatuation ends, the real work in marriage begins!

One author writes,

Maria and Ben have been married for ten years. The couple often argues about money. For Maria, a Filipina, it is important she contribute to her younger brother's education. There are also cousins who need help and Maria feels obliged to help them, too. For Ben, an American, this is a luxury the couple cannot afford. When finances get tight, the first argument is usually about the money that is sent away. Nothing gets resolved and resentments simmer. Ben finds it difficult to understand the strong obligation Maria has toward her family and Maria finds it equally hard to understand Ben's lack of concern and help toward family. Both feel angry and confused.

Couples like Maria and Ben have the added challenge of discerning the role of culture when tensions occur and differences arise. Knowing "where culture leaves off and person begins" is probably one of the toughest yet most important challenges for this couple and others like them. Cultural values are so much a part of who we are that sometimes we discover the value only when it has been threatened.[10]

A helpful principle to remember when facing communication issues is this:

Do not let kindness and truth leave you;
Bind them around your neck,
Write them on the tablet of your heart. (Proverbs 3:3)

As you communicate with your spouse on a daily basis, keep this principle of "wearing kindness and truth" on your mind and in your heart. Catalin and I have a plaque in our master bathroom that serves as an excellent reminder to me of God's plan for marriage. It simply says,

Love always protects.
Love always trusts.
Love always hopes.
Love always perseveres.
Love never fails. (1 Corinthians 13:7–8)

On days when I feel discouraged, the simple truths of this plaque remind me of the vow I took to my husband and to God. I'm reminded that true love *always* protects, trusts, hopes, and perseveres, even if I may not feel like doing those things at the moment. I'm reminded that when the temporary emotions of hurt and frustration pass, my love for Catalin and for God will remain.

In his book *Cracking the Communication Code*, author and Christian counselor Dr. Emerson Eggerichs notes that he struggled for years to understand the communication problems of his clients until he finally recognized what he calls "The Crazy Cycle" of marital conflict.

He recognized these parallel truths about married couples:

WITHOUT LOVE, THE WOMAN
REACTS WITHOUT RESPECT.

WITHOUT RESPECT, THE MAN
REACTS WITHOUT LOVE.[11]

As the husband fails to love his wife and the wife fails to respect her husband, the "crazy cycle" repeats itself, leading the couple deeper into a downward spiral of negativity, despair, frustration, and unmet needs. The more disrespected the husband feels, the more love he withholds from his wife. The more unloved the wife feels, the more she disrespects her husband.

How can we break this destructive cycle? By recognizing that our responses of both love and respect to our spouse should be based on the principles of God's Word. Our response (of either love or respect) should *not* be based on our spouse's words, actions, attitudes, performance, failures, or successes. As a wife, do I love my husband? Absolutely. Am I commanded to *respect* him even if he does not act in a loving way toward me? Absolutely.

Does my husband respect me? Absolutely. Is he commanded to *love* me even if I don't act with respect toward him? Absolutely.

I recommend the following books to help facilitate communication between intercultural couples:

- *Cracking the Communication Code: The Secret to Speaking Your Mate's Language* by Dr. Emerson Eggerichs

- *Covenant Marriage: Building Communication & Intimacy* by Dr. Gary Chapman

- *The New Eve* by Robert Lewis with Jeremy Royal Howard

- *Now You're Speaking My Language: Honest Communication and Deeper Intimacy for a Stronger Marriage* by Dr. Gary Chapman

- *You Just Don't Understand: Women and Men in Conversation* by Deborah Tannen

- *That's Not What I Meant!* by Deborah Tannen

- *Third Culture Kids: The Experience of Growing Up Between Worlds (Second Revised Edition)* by David C. Pollock and Ruth E. Van Reken

- *Men Are from Mars, Women Are from Venus* by Dr. John Gray

In Scripture, husbands are commanded, "Husbands, love your wives and do not be embittered against them" (Colossians 3:19). Ephesians 5:33 (NIV) exhorts, "Each one of you also must love his wife as he loves himself, and the wife must respect her husband."

What exactly does it mean for wives to respect their husbands? In his groundbreaking book *Love and Respect*, Dr. Emerson Eggerichs writes, "There are many ways to show your husband respect. Just look for ways to appreciate his desire to protect and provide, especially when things aren't going too well for him." He offers this poignant example:

Dr. E. V. Hill, a dynamic minister who served as senior pastor of Mt. Zion Missionary Baptist Church in Los Angeles, lost his wife, Jane, to cancer a few years ago. At her funeral, Dr. Hill described some of the ways she had made him a better man. As a struggling young preacher, E. V. had trouble earning a living. E. V. came home one night and found the house dark. When he opened the door, he saw that Jane had prepared a candlelight dinner for two. He thought that was a great idea and went into the bathroom to wash his hands. He tried unsuccessfully to turn on the light. Then he felt his way into the bedroom and flipped another switch. Darkness prevailed. The young pastor went back to the dining room and asked Jane why the electricity was off. She began to cry.

"You work so hard, and we're trying," said Jane, "but it's pretty rough. I didn't have enough money to pay the light bill. I didn't want you to know about it, so I thought we would just eat by candlelight."

Dr. Hill described his wife's words with intense emotion. "She could have said, 'I've never been in this situation before. I was reared in the home of Dr. Caruthers, and we never had our lights cut off.' She could have broken my spirit; she could have ruined me; she could have demoralized me. But instead she said, 'Somehow or other we'll get these lights back on. But tonight let's eat by candlelight.'"[12]

Jane's kindness and respect toward her husband bring to mind one of my favorite Scripture passages:

He has told you, O man, what is good;
And what does the Lord require of you
But to do justice, to love kindness,
And to walk humbly with your God? (Micah 6:8)

We, as husbands and wives, honor the Lord and each other when we seek to do justice, love kindness, and walk humbly with our God. When we do so, our intercultural communication will be effective and seasoned with grace.

QUOTES *for reflection*

O Lord, who may abide in Your tent?
Who may dwell on Your holy hill?
He who walks with integrity, and works righteousness,
And speaks truth in his heart.
● Psalm 15:1–2

Who is the man who desires life
And loves length of days that he may see good?
Keep your tongue from evil
And your lips from speaking deceit.
Depart from evil and do good;
Seek peace and pursue it.
● Psalm 34:12–14

MOVIES *to watch*

Fireproof
starring Kirk Cameron
and Erin Bethea
(2008, Rated PG)

Freedom Writers
starring Hilary Swank
and Patrick Dempsey
(2007, Rated PG-13)

Hitch
starring Will Smith
and Eva Mendes
(2005, Rated PG-13)

5 [Coming to Terms with Terms with Faith and Values]

MAN IS THE ONLY animal that laughs and weeps; for he is the only animal that is struck with the difference between what things are and what they ought to be.

[William Hazlett¹]

W e derive the English word *value* from the Latin term *valere*, which means "to be worth."[2] Our values indicate what matters to us—what we consider to be right and wrong, good and evil, positive and negative, true and false, important and superficial. Our values are part of what makes us an engaged member of our culture. They also help to define and shape who we are as a person. The way we dress and act, our personal choices, our emotional outlook on life, and our spiritual lives are all influenced by our values.

But what exactly is a value? By definition, a value is

- That quality of a thing according to which it is thought of as being more or less desirable, useful, estimable, important, etc.; worth or the degree of worth

- That which is desirable or worthy of esteem for its own sake; thing or quality having intrinsic worth

- The social principles, goals, or standards held or accepted by an individual, class, society, etc.[3]

The authors of the book *In Love But Worlds Apart* write:

Our values are the basis for why certain behaviors are important to us. In each culture, these values are woven together in a unique way. To find out the underlying values that dictate your own behavior, or why this behavior is important to you, you need to ask yourself a sequence of at least three questions:

- Why do I do a certain thing in a particular way?
- Why did I give that answer?
- And why did I give that reason for that answer?[4]

Even a seemingly simple situation in which a loving wife makes a special dinner for her husband but he doesn't say "Thank you" can create conflict, tension, and feelings of frustration for a couple. By the same token, if a loving husband makes the effort to go to work each day and complete items on his "honey-do" list but his wife never shows him any appreciation, he may become frustrated as well.

In relation to the three questions above, we could ask both husband and wife *why* they feel disappointed in these situations. They would probably answer that neither of them feels appreciated. If we probed further and asked why they feel it's important to be shown appreciation, they might say that this makes them feel affirmed and significant as people. So when either spouse fails to show appreciation, the other feels devalued and this causes disappointment and frustration—which usually results in negative words and behaviors. Both feel that their deeply held values have been trampled on.

Author Dugan Romano writes: "It can usually be said that when couples are in conflict, it is because they are operating from within two different value systems that are not in agreement. . . . Values are the great intangible. People speak of the importance of having the same values in marriage but become tongue-tied when it comes to expressing just what their own values are. They often recognize what values or beliefs they hold dear only when one of these has been stepped on."[5]

She continues, "Couples with similar values generally have a greater likelihood of marital compatibility, no matter what their cultural differences might be. The problem is that many couples have similar values in some domains but not in others, which they may not realize until they are well into the marriage."[6]

Many intercultural couples assume that as long as both partners are Christians, they'll share the same moral values and spiritual beliefs. This isn't necessarily true, however. Intercultural couples often grapple with differences in their core values and beliefs regarding the following issues:

- abortion, contraception, pregnancy, infertility treatment, and deciding how many children to have
- alcohol and drug use
- baptism
- circumcision
- communion
- cutting hair, wearing makeup, wearing jewelry, and style of dress
- dancing
- dating/courtship
- death (including cremation and burial rites) and related issues, including euthanasia
- health care
- heaven and hell
- illness and its treatment
- justice and law enforcement
- salvation
- sexuality and intimacy
- tithing/financial giving

The longer a couple is married, the more differences they will identify in their values and beliefs in the areas listed above, as well as many more. Value differences cause some of the most frustrating conflicts in intercultural marriage (as well as same-culture marriage). This is because our parents and our culture begin to ingrain those values in us from the moment we are born. Unlike personal preferences (say, vanilla versus choco-late), we hold values at a much deeper and more fundamental level. If asked to define our values, most of us would not be able to define them very well because they are so deeply held, so sacred, and so foundational to our being that we rarely ex-amine or question them unless a value conflict forces us to.

To take an example, as I have mentioned previously, most evangelical Christians in Romania are very conservative. The women always wear skirts or dresses, and they wear head cov-erings in church. They do not wear makeup, jewelry, or perfume. Many older church members (and some younger ones, too) be-lieve that dancing and using birth control are sinful practices.

In contrast, in America, I do not always wear dresses, and I don't wear head coverings in church. I wear makeup, jewelry, and perfume. I love dancing, and I believe that using birth con-trol for family planning is perfectly fine. My husband recognizes that in America most Christians do not hold exactly the same views as Christians in Romania, and he allows me the freedom to live in context of my own culture. When I visit Romania and attend church with my husband, I wear a dress and a head cov-ering, and I do not wear makeup or jewelry. In that way, I re-spect his culture's more conservative values and beliefs.

Here's another example: in America, most people are not afraid of being harmed by the police. If a man's car stalls, a woman's purse is stolen, or a person otherwise needs help and sees a policeman nearby, that person would very likely ask the policeman for help. I've been in several situations in which I have asked a policeman to help me, or when a policeman has volunteered to help me. In contrast, in some nations, people are deeply fearful of the police, and for good reason. This typically is the case in countries where the police are brutal, corrupt, or part of a governmental agency or secret force that uses scare tactics, informants, and even torture to control people.

One of my former professors at Dallas Theological Semi-nary, Dr. Oscar Lopez, hails from Guatemala. He married a woman named Peggy from South Carolina who had been a mis-sionary to Guatemala. One day, Oscar and Peggy entered a small grocery store in Guatemala. They chose several items to purchase, and after the cashier told them the total, Peggy laid the correct amount of money on the counter. Dr. Lopez was aghast. Quickly, he snatched up the money and handed it to the lady. He told Peggy, "You *hand* the money to the lady. You don't lay it on the counter."

One American wife found that her German husband washed his face with cold water and brushed his teeth with hot water. To her, this was mystifying, as she had always washed her face with warm water and brushed her teeth with cold water.

At his summer job in Canada, Gordon's boss thought he was dishonest and lazy because Gordon never looked anyone in the eye. But where Gordon had grown up in Africa, children always kept their eyes to the ground when talking with adults.[7]

The Vital Value List: Questions to Ask before Getting Married

I've created a list of questions that will help you determine your values and discover how you and your loved one approach life. Based on my research and personal experience, the answers to these questions will help determine your compatibility and the level of conflict you will potentially face with your partner over differences in values and beliefs.

First, ask yourself these questions and write down your answers. Be honest. If you're not sure of any answer, or if you feel that you're just selecting the answers that you WANT to be characteristic of you, ask a trusted friend or family member to answer the questions about you. Then ask your significant other the same questions. Be sure to record his or her answers and review them carefully. Discuss them together at your earliest opportunity. Every difference has the potential for causing conflict in your marriage.

- Do you consider yourself an optimist, a pessimist, a realist, or something else? Why? If your friends, family members, and coworkers had to place you into one of these categories, what would they say? (Go ahead and ask them—you might be surprised!)

- Are you typically a positive person or a negative person? When you are placed into a situation, is your first response generally to find what is positive or to see the problems in the situation? Why do you think you tend to respond this way?

- Does your culture tend to focus more on the past, the present, or the future? Is there more emphasis on "being" (living for the present, investing in personal relationships) or on "doing" (living for the future, focusing on achievements, career goals, and financial security)?

- If you had to develop a life motto, what would it be?

- If you could offer a motto or proverb representing the overall attitude/worldview of your culture, what would it be? Many cultures have a defining proverb.

- Do others consider you friendly and outgoing (extroverted) or reserved, quiet, or shy (introverted)? How do you see yourself?

- Do you enjoy exercising? How often do you exercise or play sports? Do you plan to continue doing these activities after you get married?

- How involved are you in your church? Do you attend every week? Do you attend Sunday school classes, Bible studies, and other events, or only the church service? Do you enjoy being involved with other church-related or missions projects?

- Do you want to have children? If so, how many, and when? Do you believe in using birth control? Would you consider adoption?

- What kinds of activities and entertainment do you like to engage in during the week? On weekends? How long do you typically work per day? How much TV do you usually watch per day? What are your hobbies?

- How many "date nights" per week or per month should we have? What types of activities would you plan for date nights?

- Do you enjoy getting together with friends and inviting people over to your home for parties, dinners, and other events? How often do you currently do this?

- What are your most important dreams and goals for your life? Where do you see yourself in the next 5, 10, 15, and 20 years?

- What do you think God has called you to do?

- In what country do you see yourself living in the future? Do you like to move often, or do you plan to stay in one place for a while?

- How do you foresee your family situation after you get married? Are you planning to ask your parents, siblings, or other family members to live with you or to stay with you for extended periods of time? In your culture, do people sometimes do this without asking permission? What are your boundaries?

- How would you describe your family of origin? How do you want your own family to be the same as your family of origin? How do you want it to be different?

- Where do you see yourself working over the next few years? Are you planning to attend school or complete another type of training before you begin working? Do you enjoy your current job? Are you planning to change jobs soon?

- Are you a night owl or an early bird (Do you like to wake up late in the morning and stay up late at night, or do you prefer to wake up early and go to bed early)? What is your daily schedule like?

- How do you typically deal with conflict? Do you tend to fight or flee confrontation?

- Are you an active or a passive person? Do you like to take charge of situations, or do you tend to hang back and allow others to take control and make decisions?

These questions will help you identify essential value differences. We all know the saying "Opposites attract," and it's true, to some extent. We are attracted to those who seem exotic and who are different from us in certain fundamental ways. Yet it's our commonalities that forge a true bond between us and keep us attracted to each other and connected as marriage partners over the years. Our faith in God and our commonalities, if we focus on them and develop them properly, are what will keep us together over the long term.

If you and your partner are opposites according to the answers to most of these questions, you will likely have some major disagreements in your marriage. But keep in mind that God has a tendency to match us with a mate who will be strong in areas where we are weak, and vice versa. God places us together with people who have pronounced differences from us as well as strong commonalities. We gain awareness, wisdom, maturity, and faith as we encounter value differences and struggle to work out those differences. At first, the rubbing together of two people with different values may feel like two pieces of rough sandpaper grating against each other, but as we continue to spend time talking about value differences and working through conflicts, we wear down the rough sand and become "more smooth" and accommodating of each other. We are stretched mentally and spiritually as we are forced to come to terms with our own cultural stereotypes, values, and beliefs and try to reconcile them with the contrasting values of our spouse. In the meantime, we also learn forgiveness.

The Iceberg of Culture

L. Robert Kohls, a cross-cultural consultant and author, suggests that culture is a kind of iceberg, with the tip visible above the surface of the water and another, much larger part, hidden below. The tip, which is visible above the water, can be identified as the *surface culture*. It includes behaviors, languages, customs, and traditions. The larger part of the iceberg, which is hidden under the water where no one can see, is the *deep culture*, which consists of the person's beliefs, values, assumptions, and thought processes that he or she rarely questions.[8] The following diagram illustrates Dr. Kohls's findings.[9]

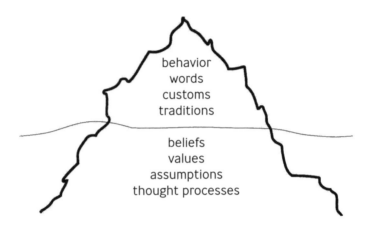

behavior
words
customs
traditions

beliefs
values
assumptions
thought processes

Some of the conflicts experienced by Dorrie and her husband, Hiroshi, demonstrate the truth of the "iceberg" cultural model. Dorrie, a Dutch woman who married a Japanese man she met in graduate school in the United States, explained that it took her many years to begin to spot the value differences that were at the bottom of most of their fights. Dorrie and Hiroshi slept on a futon, a Japanese-style mattress pad, which they hung out to air as often as possible. Because they lived in an apartment, Dorrie always hung the futon mattress and quilts over the balcony "with the side we sleep on facing out to get the most air and sun." But Hiroshi regularly berated her for not hanging them with the "pretty side" out for others to see. He was more interested in appearance and was concerned about the impression they would make on their neighbors, while Dorrie felt that it was more important for the used side of the bedding to get fresh air and sunlight. Behind this conflict were two different sets of cultural values.[10]

Dugan Romano notes that it doesn't take much for seemingly

minor issues like this to become major ones. She writes, "Couples begin talking about the two sides of a futon and escalate into slinging negative remarks at one another regarding the other's bad (different) upbringing, desire for control, or other irritation. Often couples never learn to identify what is actually behind the conflict. They never learn to recognize or empathize with the other's viewpoint or the history behind it. They think they are fighting about futons."[11]

One of my favorite restaurants is a nearby Mexican place called Cristina's. Catalin and I enjoy eating there and talking with the fantastic staff, most of whom are Mexican. I often stop by Cristina's to grab a bite while working on a writing project. In talking with the servers about their dreams, careers, families, and so on, I realized that the American culture and the Latin culture vary significantly in certain aspects. I tend to approach life with a "Carpe diem" attitude, with the perspective that *life is short*. I work hard to squeeze the most out of life and to live it to the fullest. Ours is a "doing" culture, so we busy ourselves with doing as much as we can now, because life is short.

I noticed that my Mexican friends, on the other hand, seem to feel that *life is long*. Why do something today when it could be put off until tomorrow? It's better to just relax and enjoy yourself today. You'll always have *mañana*. Cultivating personal relationships and having fun are elevated to the highest level, while seeking a better education, a higher-paying job, or striving for greater personal achievements take a backseat. Just *being* is the most important thing.

I understand this perspective and, in many ways, I like it! I treasure the friendship of these hardworking people. I admire their fun-loving ways, their passion, their commitment to their families, and their fierce loyalty to their friends. Their attitude is refreshing to me in many ways. My husband says, "That's just because they're young. All young people have that attitude!" He does have a point.

Yet most Americans were simply raised with a different value system. Farrah Gray, a brilliant young American entrepreneur, said, "Successful people do *today* what other people put off until tomorrow." This encapsulates a strongly Western attitude about the importance of having a strong work ethic and being willing to sacrifice certain pleasures today in order to achieve a positive result tomorrow. We call this *delayed gratification*.

One author writes, "There will be times you may feel quite ready to argue that the way *your* culture did things is biblical. The point is that cultural differences exist, and you will be forced to face some of those mentioned and many that are not mentioned. If you choose to marry interculturally, you will need to learn to face cultural differences as a reality and not deny them."[12] At times, you may be tempted to use the Bible to support your personal or cultural preferences. Keep in mind that certain teachings that were relevant at the time that the Bible was written may not be relevant now, and they may not be upheld by all cultures in the twenty-first century. Examples of these could include certain dietary restrictions, women remaining silent in church, or rituals relating to "cleanness" and "uncleanness."

Differences in values and worldviews from culture to culture can cause a crisis for a "third culture" kid or adult who is forced to constantly adjust his or her value system to fit that of a new culture. Often, these individuals begin to feel that they don't really fit into any one culture or value system. Like people dressing up for a costume party, they keep trying on different masks, not sure which one to wear at which times. One "third culture kid" wrote the following poem about his experience:

I am
a confusion of cultures.
Uniquely me.
I think this is good
because I can
understand
the traveler, sojourner, foreigner,
the homesickness
that comes.

I think this is also bad
because I cannot
be understood
by the person who has sown and grown in one place.
They know not
the real meaning of homesickness
that hits me
now and then.
Sometimes I despair of
understanding them.
I am
an island
and
a United Nations.
Who can recognise either
in me but God?[13]

Love, grace, and compassion represent the "big three" attitudes that will enable intercultural couples to deal well with value differences. Remember that each individual most likely has experienced pain as he or she has tried to bridge cultures and overcome his or her personality and cultural differences to assimilate into the other person's culture.

Lastly, keep in mind that husbands and wives aren't enemies. We are not in a battle against each other; *we are on the same team*. God is on that team as well, wanting all of us to succeed and giving us the grace we need to honor our sacred covenant of marriage.

QUOTE *for reflection*

*Do not store up for yourselves treasures on earth,
where moth and rust destroy, and where thieves break
in and steal. But store up for yourselves treasures in
heaven, where neither moth nor rust destroys, and
where thieves do not break in or steal; for where
your treasure is, there your heart will be also.*

●Matthew 6:19–21

MOVIES *to watch*

Anna and the King
starring Jodie Foster
and Chow Yun-Fat
(1999, Rated PG-13)

New in Town
starring Renee Zellweger
and Harry Connick Jr.
(2009, Rated PG)

Shadowlands
starring Debra Winger
and Anthony Hopkins
(1993, Rated PG)

6 [A Biblical Look at Intercultural Marriage]

OFTEN THE DIFFERENCE between a successful marriage and a mediocre one consists of leaving about three or four things a day unsaid.

[HARLAN MILLER[1]]

The more research I have done on intercultural marriage, the more I have realized that it has long been misunderstood by Christians. For thousands of years, scriptural principles have been misinterpreted and twisted to accommodate people's racial biases, prejudices, and personal agendas.

Perhaps the strongest misconception I've found is the idea that intercultural and interracial marriage were prohibited by God for racial, ethnic, or cultural reasons. This is *not* the case. Some of the wisest and most honored biblical heroes and heroines (including Moses, David, Esther, Ruth, Solomon, and Joseph) were involved in intercultural or interracial marriages—marriages that God approved of and blessed.

The Bible does contain some instances in which God warns His people not to intermarry with others, but this was *always* for spiritual reasons rather than for racial or cultural reasons. He wanted His people to keep themselves spiritually pure by not marrying people who worshipped idols or who engaged in other pagan practices. God does not prohibit marriage (intercultural or otherwise) except when it involves a Christian marrying a person who is not a Christian (2 Corinthians 6:14).

One author on the Web site Bible.org writes,

> God forbade the Israelites to intermarry with the Canaanites—the people of the land. (See Genesis 24:3; 28:1; Exodus 34:10–17; Deuteronomy 7:3; Joshua 23:12–13;

Ezra 9:2ff.) But intermarriage with all so-called foreigners was not prohibited (see Deuteronomy 21:10–13). We
should recall that a number of foreigners (non-Israelites,
by race) were a part of the promised line of Messiah, including Tamar (Genesis 38), Rahab (Joshua 2:1ff.), and
Ruth (Book of Ruth). . . . Then there were the foreign
wives of Solomon, which led to his downfall (1 Kings 11).
It was not so much a matter of these women being
foreign (non-Jewish by race), but a matter of these
women worshipping foreign gods that was at issue. The
concern was always that men's hearts would be turned
from God to idols.

He continues, "In the New Testament, marrying an unbeliever (no matter what race) was forbidden (1 Corinthians 7:39;
2 Corinthians 6:14–18). It seems very clear that faith in Jesus
Christ tears down racial barriers. . . . If marriage is a picture of
the relationship of Jesus Christ to His bride, the church (all
true believers), then marriage to a believer of another race simply pictures the fact that Jesus came to save Gentiles as well as
Jews."[2]

God used marriage as the ultimate example of how faith,
love, and grace can bring together believers of all races, tribes,
and languages through a shared belief in Jesus Christ.

Intercultural Marriage in History

Intercultural marriage has existed almost since the beginning of mankind. After the incident that occurred at the Tower
of Babel, people were scattered over the face of the earth (Genesis 11:1–9). As the years passed, various language dialects, traditions, and cultural habits developed that were particular to
people groups who migrated to different areas. People began to
consider their own language and ways as familiar and right,
and other languages and traditions as "foreign."

Over the years since then, many nations of the world have
had regulations banning or restricting intercultural and interracial marriage. During the Nazi regime, Germany banned
interracial marriage, and South Africa also banned it during

the apartheid era. Intercultural and interracial marriage were illegal in most areas of the United States until the 1967 Supreme Court ruling in the case of *Loving v. Virginia*. In this case, Richard Loving, a white man, was convicted under Virginia's anti-miscegenation law for marrying Mildred Jeter, a woman of African American and Native American descent. On appeal of this conviction, Loving argued that the law violated the Fourteenth Amendment of the Constitution, which requires that all citizens receive equal treatment under the law. In a unanimous decision, the Supreme Court found in the couple's favor, proclaiming the Virginia statute unconstitutional.[3]

Intercultural and Interracial Marriages in the Bible

Now, let's take a look at several biblical marriage narratives. Most of them are poignant love stories, but a few are cautionary tales. From these biblical examples, we'll discover more about God's gift of marriage and the intriguing dynamics of intercultural partnerships.

Moses and Zipporah

Moses' sister, Miriam, and his brother, Aaron, spoke out against Moses in part because they disapproved of the Cushite woman, Zipporah, whom he had married (Numbers 12:1). Zipporah was the daughter of Jethro, the priest of the land of Midian. Most biblical scholars agree that the region called *Cush* was located in what is now Ethiopia, meaning that Zipporah was most likely black.

Notice that God never told Moses not to marry Zipporah. The fact that she was black seemed to be a non-issue, and her godly religious heritage as the daughter of a priest made her an excellent match for Moses. However, Miriam and Aaron grew jealous, not only of the fact that Moses had married a woman who was not an Israelite, but of the fact that God had chosen to use Moses as His mouthpiece when speaking to the people. Miriam and Aaron used the fact that Moses had married a Cushite woman to try to stir up the Israelites to question his authority and mutiny against his leadership.

God responded sternly to Miriam and Aaron's sinful racial and cultural prejudice as well as their attempt to undermine Moses' leadership. According to Numbers 12:9–10, God struck Miriam with leprosy as a result of her choice to speak out against Moses and Zipporah. (Most likely, Aaron would have been struck with leprosy, too, if not for the Jewish law that a priest could not be a leper.) Moses prayed fervently for God to heal Miriam. The Lord decreed that, because Miriam was unclean, she must stay outside the Israelites' camp for seven days. After that time, He restored her health. Both Miriam and Aaron learned a valuable lesson about racial prejudice. As far as we know, they did not speak out against Moses and Zipporah ever again.

Samson and Delilah

Samson began life as a Nazirite, set apart from birth for the purpose of serving God. An angel visited Samson's mother before his birth and told her that Samson was not to drink wine, eat unclean food, or have his hair cut as he grew up. But one day, when he was a young man, Samson saw a beautiful Philistine woman in Timnah. He told his father and mother, "Get her for me as a wife."

His parents protested and said, "Is there no woman among the daughters of your relatives, or among all our people, that you go to take a wife from the uncircumcised Philistines?" But Samson said to his father, "Get her for me, for she looks good to me" (Judges 14:2–3).

Any red flags there? Samson knew nothing about this woman except the fact that she was beautiful and she came from the tribe of the Philistines, the Jews' arch-enemies, who worshipped idols. Samson married her, and she betrayed him. Her father gave her to Samson's friend as a wife (Judges 14:20). When Samson discovered this, he was furious. He retaliated against the Philistines by burning their crops. As a result of the destruction that Samson's wife had brought to them by marrying Samson, the Philistines put Samson's wife, her father, and the rest of her family to death.

After that time, Samson judged Israel for twenty years

(Judges 15:20). But he hadn't learned his lesson about lusting after women who did not serve the Lord. He fell in love with a woman named Delilah from the Valley of Sorek, which separated the land of Judah from the land of the Philistines. The Philistines coerced Delilah to get Samson to reveal to her the source of his strength. Three times he told her the wrong answer. Finally, however, he revealed the truth: that if his hair were cut, he would lose his strength. During the night, Delilah called a man to come and cut off Samson's hair (Judges 16:5–19).

The next morning, the Philistines seized Samson, gouged out his eyes, and forced him to work as a grinder in the prison. The Philistines also made sport of Samson, forcing him to entertain them at parties. But his hair grew while he was in prison, and his strength began to return. Samson's last act was to use a massive show of strength to bring down the pillars of a large house where the Philistines were celebrating. Samson died when the house collapsed, along with 3,000 Philistines (Judges 16:20–31).

Samson's downfall was his weakness for women who did not love and serve God. His example offers a strong warning for us, demonstrating why a Christian should not marry a person who doesn't share the same faith or spiritual values.

David and Bathsheba

King David's love affair with Bathsheba is one of the Bible's best-known stories of intrigue. Bathsheba was the daughter of Eliam and the wife of Uriah the Hittite, one of David's "mighty men"—his band of thirty-seven fierce and loyal warriors.

The Hittites were a pagan tribe related to the Canaanites. The Bible authors contrast the sinful actions of the Jewish king David with the godly and honorable actions of this Gentile and formerly pagan man named Uriah, who evidently had converted to the Jewish faith.

David sinned by committing adultery with Bathsheba, who became pregnant. Then David had Uriah killed in battle so he could marry her (2 Samuel 11). As a result of this sin, the child born to David and Bathsheba died. However, they later bore a son named Solomon who gained great favor, renown, and wisdom from the Lord. Jesus, the Messiah, was part of the lineage of David, Bathsheba, and Solomon.

Solomon and the Shulammite Woman

Solomon, the son of David and Bathsheba, shared a great love with a young, beautiful Shulammite girl. We read this heartwarming love story in the book of Song of Solomon. Scripture says that the girl was dark-skinned, in part because of the work she had to do in the fields. But she may also have been of African or Egyptian descent.

The Song of Solomon is one of the most poignant love stories in all of literature. As intercultural couples, we can learn a great deal about love, conflict, conflict resolution, intimacy, and more by reading it. Engaged couples may enjoy reading this book on their wedding night.

We don't know what ever happened to the Shulammite girl, but the Bible indicates that, in later life, Solomon became involved with a wide variety of women from pagan backgrounds who led him away from the Lord. He may have been influenced by his father's philandering with Bathsheba and other women.

However, every couple can learn important lessons by reading the book of Song of Solomon together. Also look for the following excellent resources on the Song of Solomon by pastor Tommy Nelson:

- *The Book of Romance: What Solomon Says about Love, Sex, and Intimacy*

- *Song of Solomon Classic DVD Series: A Study of Love, Marriage, Sex, and Romance*

Ahasuerus and Esther (also called Xerxes)

The pagan King Xerxes selected an exquisite young woman named Esther from among the most beautiful young women in the land to become his queen in place of the former Queen Vashti.

At the recommendation of her cousin Mordecai, Esther

kept her Jewish heritage a secret during the selection process and after she had become queen. However, the king's right-hand man, Haman, hatched a plot to destroy all of the Jews because Mordecai refused to bow down to him. Mordecai informed Esther of Haman's sinister plot and told her, "Do not imagine that you in the king's palace can escape any more than all the Jews. For if you remain silent at this time, relief and deliverance will arise for the Jews from another place and you and your father's house will perish. And who knows whether you have not attained royalty for such a time as this?" (Esther 4: 13–14).

Esther courageously approached the king to plead for the lives of her people. He allowed them to defend themselves against their enemies, and he ordered Haman to be hung on the gallows that Haman had built for Mordecai. Esther provides a powerful example for women who have married a man from another culture or belief system. She responded to her husband with respect and honor, and he honored her and her people in return.

Boaz and Ruth

Ruth hailed from the land of Moab, east of the Dead Sea. After the death of her husband, Mahlon, Ruth demonstrated remarkable loyalty and courage by staying with her Israelite mother-in-law, Naomi, who had also been recently widowed (Ruth 1:16). Ruth traveled with Naomi back to Naomi's hometown of Bethlehem in the land of Judah.

Naomi and Ruth's arrival created quite a stir in Bethlehem. The Moabite people were often in conflict with the Israelites, so no doubt people were surprised at Ruth's choice to enter the land of Judah with Naomi.

Ruth "happened" to glean in a field owned by a wealthy and benevolent man named Boaz. He immediately noticed that she was a foreigner and offered her protection in his fields. As Boaz watched Ruth glean day by day, he recognized her excellent and noble character.

Naomi advised Ruth to go down to the threshing floor at night and let Boaz know that he could serve as a kinsman-redeemer for her. She did so and asked him to spread his garment over her as an indication that he would marry her and provide for her (Ruth 3:9).

Ruth and Boaz married and had a son named Obed, the father of Jesse, who became the father of King David in the line of Christ (Ruth 4:17).

Joseph and Asenath

We don't know much about this partnership, but Joseph, son of the patriarch Jacob, gained favor with the Pharaoh of Egypt. As a result, Joseph was given Asenath, the daughter of an Egyptian priest, as a wife (Genesis 41:45). Asenath was a dark-skinned beauty from a culture that held views that contrasted with the traditions and religious heritage of the Jews. However, because Joseph was an honorable man who had gained great favor even from foreign kings, he most likely was able to strike a balance between his own faith and values and those of his wife. Joseph and Asenath bore two sons, Manasseh and Ephraim (Genesis 46:20).

A Summary of Biblical Teaching on Intercultural Marriage

Pastor and author John Piper lists the following biblical principles on race and racial harmony, which also apply directly to intercultural marriage:

- God designed all ethnic groups from one human ancestor. (Acts 17:26)

- All members of every ethnic group are made in the image of God. (Genesis 1:27)

- In determining the significance of who you are, being a person in the image of God compares to ethnic distinctives the way the light of the noonday sun compares to the light from the candles on a birthday cake. Being a person is infinitely more significant than being a white person or a black person.

- The prediction of a curse that Noah spoke over some of the descendents of Ham is irrelevant in deciding how the black race is to be viewed and treated. Ham's descendents were Canaanites, not Africans. (Genesis 10:15-18)

- It is God's purpose and command that we make disciples for Jesus Christ from every ethnic group in the world, without distinction. (Matthew 28:18-20)

- All believers in Jesus Christ, of every ethnic group, are united to each other not only in common humanity in the image of God, but even more, as brothers and sisters in Christ and members of the same body. (Romans 12:4-5)

- The Bible forbids intermarriage between believer and unbeliever, but not between members of different ethnic groups. (1 Corinthians 7:39)

- Therefore, against the spirit of indifference, alienation, and hostility in our land, let us embrace the supremacy of God's love to take new steps personally and corporately toward racial harmony, expressed visibly in our communities and in our churches.[4]

Male and Female Roles

Western societies tend to be more egalitarian than others in their views of the roles of men and women, but gender inequalities remain in every society. Tradition, religious beliefs, politics, social class, and caste also may influence a couple's understanding of male and female roles.

In most areas of the U.S. and in many Western countries, the class system is less pronounced, but other cultures (such as the Indian culture) adhere to a strict class and caste system that greatly influences each person's interactions with others. Intercultural couples must explore this issue to form a better understanding of each spouse's attitudes toward roles and class. As husbands and wives engage in open discussion, they will learn to sort out cultural stereotypes, personal expectations, and biblical principles in order to reach a workable, God-honoring partnership in which each individual respects the other's roles.

According to Scripture, the husband is commanded to show submission to the Lord Jesus Christ by loving his wife and showing her honor (Colossians 3:19; 1 Peter 3:7). The wife is responsible to submit to the husband (Ephesians 5:24) and to respect him. In addition, all believers are commanded to submit to each other (Ephesians 5:21). This means that as Christians, both men and women are to model submission, as Christ did.

Together with your fiancé or spouse, read Ephesians 5 and discuss the marriage principles that you find. How does your culture interpret the roles of men and women? How did your parents interpret them? How were these roles modeled (or not modeled) in your family of origin? Be sure to ask your loved one the same questions.

One book that will help you define and create workable marriage roles is *Rocking the Roles* by Robert Lewis and William Hendricks.

Marital Intimacy

A man falls in love through his eyes; a woman, through her ears. —Woodrow Wyatt[5]

Before a couple commits to an intercultural marriage, each partner should discover the facts about his or her loved one's intimate past as well as his or her attitudes toward sex and intimacy. This can be a difficult task, as sexuality is still considered a taboo subject in many cultures, especially among Christians.

Some questions to ask before marriage are

- What is your culture's view toward intimacy before marriage?
- What is your culture's view toward intimacy after marriage?

- What are your personal beliefs on these issues?

- What did your family teach about these issues?

- What has been your intimate or sexual involvement before our engagement/marriage?

- What do you expect our intimate life to be like after we are married?

- What do you expect our intimate life to be like during pregnancy? Does your culture have certain traditions or rules about this?

- What do you expect our intimate life to be like after we have children?

- What will we do to keep our love life strong?

Christian resources, including books, videos, and conferences, like the Intimate Issues Conferences and FamilyLife Conferences, can help couples expand their knowledge and improve their intimate relationship. For more information about the Intimate Issues conference for women, visit www.intimateissues.com. Linda Dillow has a book for women also called *Intimate Issues* that I highly recommend. For more information about the fantastic, truly life-transforming "Weekend to Remember" marriage conferences sponsored by FamilyLife, please see www.familylife.com.

QUOTES *for reflection*

The Shulammite Woman:
May he kiss me with the kisses of his mouth!
for your love is better than wine . . .
I am black but lovely,
O daughters of Jerusalem.
●Song of Solomon 1:2, 5

Solomon:
To me, my darling, you are like
My mare among the chariots of Pharaoh.
Your cheeks are lovely with ornaments,
Your neck with strings of beads.
How beautiful you are, my darling,
How beautiful you are!
Your eyes are like doves.
●Song of Solomon 1:9–11, 15

(

MOVIES *to watch*

Australia
starring Nicole Kidman
and Hugh Jackman
(2008, Rated PG-13)

One Night with the King
starring Tiffany Dupont
and Luke Goss
(2006, Rated PG)

Under the Tuscan Sun
starring Diane Lane
and Raoul Bova
(2003, Rated PG-13)

7 [Getting a Grip on Time]

ENJOY YOURSELF. It's later than you think.

[CHINESE PROVERB]

"Time is money."

"The early bird catches the worm."

"A stitch in time saves nine."

"Early to bed, early to rise, makes a man healthy, wealthy, and wise."

These phrases and proverbs, so common in American culture, illustrate that our attitude toward time exerts a tremendous influence on us. We may not be aware of our perception of time, yet we naturally interpret events, attitudes, situations, and behavior according to our cultural understandings of it. Because our view of time is so deep-seated and fundamental to our being, we rarely recognize it until something happens to make us reevaluate that view. Often, intercultural marriage serves as that catalyst, sending a shock through our system as we realize that our own time values differ significantly from those of our intercultural spouse.

In his book *Mixed Matches*, Dr. Joel Crohn notes that the following six cultural dimensions serve as a crucial framework for understanding differences in intercultural marriage:

- Time
- The nature of the universe
- The cohesiveness of the family
- Emotional expressiveness
- Interpersonal relations
- Gender roles[1]

Time appears first here as one of the most important building blocks within our cultural framework. Most Western cultures possess a *linear* concept of time, while others conceive of time as more *generational* or *cyclical.* Interestingly, every culture on earth evaluates life primarily through one of three main "lenses": the lens of the past, the present, or the future.

Naturally, every culture will contain *some* elements of all three perspectives, but will be identified primarily by one. We could say that each culture has a "most-valued," "secondary," and "least-valued" form.[2] For example, to make a broad generalization, America, Britain, and most countries in Western Europe are "future oriented," while some Latin and European cultures could be described as "present oriented" (such as those in Mexico and southern Italy), and some Native American and Asian cultures could be considered "past oriented." The following chart will help you understand the differences between the three conceptualizations of time:

	PAST	PRESENT	FUTURE
TIME	Remember the past; honor your family's traditions and cultural history.	Enjoy today; that's what's most important.	Always think ahead and plan for tomorrow.[3]

Author Dugan Romano notes that the question *How late is late?* is answered in different ways in different cultures, and being on time is assigned much more value in certain cultures than others.[4] In the U.S. and other Western nations, for example, people tend to concern themselves with punctuality and schedules. Because Western cultures are future-oriented, their people want to *save* time. People in these cultures base their lives on the hope of future growth and success, and every moment counts toward making that future happen.

Western culture can be defined by some of its popular maxims, such as "Every second counts." In future-oriented societies, people measure time in small increments: hours, minutes, and seconds. The obsession with time, rather than being a celebration of the moment, is an attempt to shape and control the future. One author notes, "To the extent that a culture is future-oriented, it stresses production, accomplishment, and accumulation of wealth."[5]

In certain other cultures that are present-oriented (for instance, in Latin America and the Middle East), more value is placed on *using* time to the fullest than *being* on time. In these cultures, people believe in the concept of *carpe diem*, or "seizing the day"—making the most of each moment by living it to the hilt and being fully present. As a rule, people from these cultures are more interested in the quality of their *present* life than in the future.[6] They recognize, and wisely so, that the future isn't guaranteed.

In more traditional, slower-paced societies like these, time is more likely to be measured in seasons rather than seconds. In these societies, people depend more highly on land, crops, and animals for their livelihood, yet they also understand that they can't control the future any more than they can control the weather. As a result, they focus on living in the present and savoring every moment of rest and pleasure, recognizing that tomorrow's labor will be here soon enough.

In these cultures, people tend to be more relaxed and unhurried, focusing on enjoying time with friends and family. They also engage in more time-consuming courtesies and conversations than people from other cultures. Even the languages of these cultures reflect this fundamental difference: in English, the word *tomorrow* means "the day after today," but the Spanish and Arabic words for *tomorrow, mañana* and *bukra*, are more vague, simply meaning "sometime in the future."[7]

In past-oriented cultures, on the other hand, people measure time by generations. Each person's actions are viewed against a grid of their ancestors' beliefs, values, and behaviors. Many families in these cultures have shrines in their homes to serve as constant reminders of the value of their traditions and family heritage.[8]

The following example illustrates the conflicts that can

occur when two people who view the world through different "time lenses" choose to marry. Helga, a German woman who married a man from Libya, described the couple's time differences this way:

> His time and my time are so different that more and more we find we are doing things separately to avoid bickering. He resents my harping at him and says I try to keep track of his movements. He won't wear a watch; says he doesn't need it. For him time is rubber; it stretches. But I go mad when he says he's going out for fifteen minutes and comes back three hours later without any explanation. I have no schedules to work my day around, can never count on him to be on time for anything—movies, parties, even dinner. He is never ever on time for dinner. He believes in eating when he's hungry![9]

Catalin and I witnessed another interesting time-related interaction recently. Our friends Elena (from Macedonia) and Gil (from Puerto Rico) called one Saturday to invite us to dinner at 8:00 p.m. that evening with a group of friends at Al-Amir, a Middle Eastern restaurant in Dallas. We arrived a few minutes after eight on Saturday evening, entered the lavish tri-level building pulsing with lively Eastern rhythms, and sat down on pillow-covered wooden benches at an unusual table with a cutout hole for our feet. Downstairs, two belly dancers whirled in filmy yellow and fuchsia costumes.

We chatted with Elena's sister, Aleksandra, as we waited for Elena and Gil to arrive. A few minutes later, they appeared and greeted us. We chatted with Gil for a few minutes while Elena excused herself to the ladies' room. "Sorry we're late," said Gil. "That's what it's like when you're married to a Macedonian!"

We both laughed, understanding completely. When Elena returned to the table, she hugged us and squeezed into the small space at the end of the table next to Gil. "I'm so sorry we're late," she said. "That's what happens when you marry a Puerto Rican!"

It all depends on your perspective, doesn't it?

It's About Time . . .

Calendars are for careful people, not passionate ones.
—Carl Sandburg

In his book *The Reflective Life*, author Ken Gire shares this story:

In a shady corner of the great market in Mexico City was an old Indian named Pota-lamo. He had twenty strings of onions hanging in front of him.

An American from Chicago came up and said:

"How much for a string of onions?"

"Ten cents," said Pota-lamo.

"How much for two strings?"

"Twenty cents," was the reply.

"How much for three strings?"

"Thirty cents," was the answer.

"Not much reduction in that," said the American. "Would you take twenty-five cents?"

"No," said the Indian.

"How much for your whole twenty strings?" said the American.

"I would not sell you my twenty strings," replied the Indian.

"Why not?" said the American. "Aren't you here to sell your onions?"

"No," replied the Indian. "I am here to live my life. I love this marketplace. I love the crowds and the red serapes. I love the sunlight and the waving palmettos. I love to have Pedro and Luis come by and say: '*Buenas dias*' . . . and talk about the babies and the crops. I love to see my friends. That is my life. For that I sit here all day and sell my twenty strings of onions. But if I sell all my onions to one customer, then is my day ended. I have lost my life that I love—and that I will not do."[10]

Clearly, the Indian man valued his time spent in the market, living his daily life among the people he loved, more than he valued the American man's money or the opportunity to quickly sell his onions. This poignant story reveals the difference between present-oriented cultures like Mexico and future-oriented ones like the United States. This man's understanding of his priorities brings to mind the compelling Scripture verse, "Teach us to number our days, that we may present to You a heart of wisdom" (Psalm 90:12).

Often in America *time is perceived as an oppressive taskmaster, while the people are the servant.* Unfortunately, Westerners (myself included) often fall victim to the "tyranny of the urgent" and let their work projects, responsibilities, and schedules push aside what's truly important: their relationships with God, their spouse, and their family and friends.

In contrast, life in many other cultures, including Romania, unfolds at a much slower pace. Graciousness and hospitality reign supreme. *Time is the servant, and people are the master.* Hosts welcome their guests warmly, treat them with the utmost respect, and offer them the best of everything. Hosts also adjust their schedules as necessary to accommodate the needs of others. If a friend or family member shows up unannounced at the door, the host immediately invites the guest inside, offers the guest a drink and a meal, and usually asks him or her to spend the night. Any plans the host may have had are changed or abandoned altogether to make room for the visit. In short, people live out the biblical command to "love your neighbor as yourself."

An expert in the law once tested Jesus by asking Him, "Teacher, which is the greatest commandment in the Law?" Jesus replied: "'Love the Lord your God with all your heart and with all your soul and with all your mind.' This is the first and greatest commandment. And the second is like it: 'Love your neighbor as yourself'" (Matthew 22:35–39 NIV). This was a radical statement then, and it's radical now. But when we commit ourselves fully to loving God and loving people, especially by taking time to care for our spouses and show hospitality even when it requires sacrifice, we'll reap the rewards of a life lived in obedience to God.

Marching to the Beat of a Different Drummer

> If a man does not keep pace with his companions, perhaps
> it is because he hears a different drummer. Let him step to
> the music which he hears, however measured or far away.
> —Henry David Thoreau

Anthropologist Edward Hall notes that just as each individual moves to his or her own distinct rhythm, so do cultures. From the moment of birth, each person has been trained to conform to certain cultural rhythms and ways of viewing the world.[11]

In some ways, every culture is like a symphony playing its own unique music according to its own rhythms. The people of that culture, the musicians, have spent their lives learning the music, and they perform it well—better than anyone else could. However, when they enter another culture and have to perform with a foreign symphony, they struggle. They've never heard the music before. They haven't had time to learn it, and they don't know how to play it. (As a violinist, I can certainly relate!) Perhaps the music is much faster, much slower, or more dissonant than the music they're used to. In addition, they feel out of their element, as they've never performed with this new group of musicians before. As a result, they must adjust to the rhythms of the other culture before they can successfully perform that culture's music.

In a scene in the movie *Dead Poets Society*, John Keating, an inspiring teacher at an all-male prep school, chooses three of his students and asks them to walk in a circle in a courtyard. At first, all three young men walk at different paces as Keating announces, "No grades at stake, gentlemen. Just take a stroll." After only a few moments, however, the three boys fall into step and begin to march in exactly the same cadence, like soldiers. The rest of the class begins to clap in rhythm. Keating remarks,

> Thank you, gentlemen. If you noticed, everyone started
> off with their own stride, their own pace . . .
> I brought them up here to illustrate the point of

conformity: the difficulty in maintaining your own beliefs in the face of others.

Now, we all have a great need for acceptance. But you must trust that your beliefs are unique, your own, even though others may think them odd or unpopular, even though the herd may go, "That's baaaaad." Robert Frost said, "Two roads diverged in a wood and I, I took the one less traveled by, and that has made all the difference."[12]

In intercultural marriage, at times, you may feel that you and your partner are "out of step" with each other or that you're walking an overgrown path. Here's the good news: that's what makes each of you unique individuals, and God made you exactly the way you are for a reason. In my own marriage, I've grown much more from wrestling with the areas in which my husband and I *don't agree* than I have from the areas in which we agree. Without opportunities to stretch our minds and mature our faith, we have no impetus to grow.

Here's another helpful way to think about time differences in marriage. If you've ever traveled overseas, you know what jet lag feels like. The sun might be radiating directly overhead, announcing that it's noon, while your body tells you in no uncertain terms that it's actually midnight and you should be in bed sleeping soundly. The disorientation, the queasiness, the exhaustion, the light-headedness, the upset stomach, the lack of appetite: I've experienced all these and more in my international journeys over the years. Thankfully, God has fashioned our bodies as marvelous creations, able to adapt to a multitude of stressful conditions. After a day or two of adjustment, our body clocks miraculously regulate to the time of the other country, and we're able to enjoy our experience more fully.

When you marry a person from a culture that possesses a different concept of time from yours, you may feel that you've developed a case of prolonged jet lag. Perhaps the "drummer" that you hear seems permanently out of step with the one your partner hears. Maybe your "symphony" has been struggling for years to learn the music of your partner's culture, with little success, as the following real-life story illustrates:

Hafsa, a woman from Morocco, struggled to adjust to the schedule of her American husband, Mike. As an airline pilot, Mike operated on a strict schedule. He timed everything, including the amount of time it took Hafsa to get to the point when she called someone on the phone. Mike was frustrated with the amount of time that he felt Moroccans wasted, and he tried to dispense with what he considered the "senseless formalities" of his wife's culture. Hafsa had her hands full trying to explain to her friends that her husband was "just being American" rather than being rude.[13]

Like Mike and Hafsa, Catalin and I have struggled somewhat with time issues. The primary issue is that, in certain cases, I seem to care more about keeping a schedule and being on time than he does, especially when meeting friends or family members. (He's always on time for work and his university classes.) I've found the following three-step process helpful in overcoming conflict in our marriage. It applies to time issues, as well. For our purposes, I will call it the FIX model (conFess, Investigate, and eXplore solutions).

First, Catalin and I 'fess up to our own emotions. Each of us asks, "How am I feeling? Why am I so upset?" And we verbalize those emotions to each other. (Remember that during this step, it's important to use the word *I* rather than *you*. Instead of accusing your spouse, simply state your own emotions: "This is how *I* feel" rather than "*You* make me feel . . .")

Now, let's put it into practice. My personal feelings with regard to the time issue might be, "I don't like to be late. I feel disappointed, frustrated, and angry when others have to wait for us. When we're late to an event, I don't enjoy myself as much because of all the stress involved before we reach our destination."

Next, I take things a step further, investigating the real root of the conflict. I ask myself, "What are my (and our) underlying personal or cultural values that may be causing the conflict?"

By doing some soul-searching, I might come up with the

following answer: "My family always valued punctuality and dependability, so I'm embarrassed to be late. I don't like to have to make excuses or apologize to others when we're late to events because I'm uncomfortable feeling judged by others. Also, I feel that being late communicates the message 'You aren't important' to my family and friends. I don't want to send them that message because I value them."

Last, we explore solutions, asking, "What can we do about it?" I've found it best to have discussions on topics like this when we aren't upset with each other. Clarifying our feelings and sharing the reasons behind them helps each of us understand the other's point of view. Usually, the "explore" step also includes apologies on both parts, praying together, and making a heartfelt decision to communicate better in the future and try to avoid conflict on the same issue.

Also, whenever possible, I seek to examine my attitudes in private and lift up my frustration to God through prayer rather than taking out that frustration on my husband. In Ephesians 5:22–24, Scripture reminds me that part of my role is to be subject to my spouse and lovingly submit to his leadership. Recently, I felt God leading me to release the responsibility for my husband's lateness and stop feeling that I have to apologize for him. This has lifted a burden from me and has helped me to have a more positive attitude about punctuality.

Gradually, my need to cling so tightly to a schedule has relaxed. I've realized that the world won't end if Catalin and I are five minutes late to meet someone at Starbucks. And if time issues ever do cause a conflict, I may just have to say, "That's what happens when you marry someone from Romania!" If some people don't understand, that's okay. I'm learning to march to the beat of my own drummer, and I'm giving my husband the freedom to do the same.

QUOTE *for reflection*

There is a time for everything,
and a season for every activity under heaven:
a time to be born and a time to die,
a time to plant and a time to uproot,
a time to kill and a time to heal,
a time to tear down and a time to build,
a time to weep and a time to laugh,
a time to mourn and a time to dance,
a time to scatter stones and a time to gather them,
a time to embrace and a time to refrain,
a time to search and a time to give up,
a time to keep and a time to throw away,
a time to tear and a time to mend,
a time to be silent and a time to speak,
a time to love and a time to hate,
a time for war and a time for peace.
He has made everything beautiful in its time.
He has also set eternity in the hearts of men . . .

• Ecclesiastes 3:1–8, 11 NIV

MOVIES *to watch*

Dead Poets Society
starring Robin Williams
and Robert Sean Leonard
(1989, Rated PG)

The Sisterhood of the Traveling Pants
starring Amber Tamblyn,
Alexis Bledel, America Ferrera,
and Blake Lively
(2005, Rated PG)

8 [Avoiding Food Fights: Resoving Food and Mealtime Issues]

THOSE WHO are at one regarding food are at one in life.

[MALAWIAN PROVERB]

Wh-en you say "I do" to a man or woman from another culture, you can be assured of at least one thing: some conflicts will arise regarding food. Dugan Romano, the author of *Intercultural Marriage: Promises & Pitfalls,* states, "No other single cultural difference was cited so often by couples as a problem as food."[1]

James Beard said, "Food is our common ground, a universal experience."[2] We all have to eat—most of us, at least three meals a day. That means that food-related conflicts can arise over and over again unless you and your spouse choose to discuss meals and mealtimes in advance and plan accordingly. This chapter will help you develop culinary common ground while you deepen your understanding of your spouse's habits, values, and preferences regarding food.

Mealtimes and the American Family

Where love sets the table, food tastes its best.
—French Proverb

During my high school and college years, I realized that my own family's traditional attitudes toward food and mealtimes varied significantly from those of other American families. My mother stayed home and cooked meals for us daily. We rarely went out to restaurants together, and we very rarely ate junk food. Mealtimes in our house involved a happy form of chaos, but we also followed certain unspoken rules. We always prayed before eating, and we were not permitted to read books or magazines or watch TV while sitting at the table. Mealtimes involved eating and bonding as a family as we shared our experiences through food, conversation, and laughter.

In twenty-first-century America, however, many families' mealtimes are much more fragmented. Individual members of the family may eat meals at different times while engaging in a variety of activities—watching TV, working on the computer, playing video games, reading magazines, or standing and talking in the kitchen. In addition, many modern women work outside the home, and their families may eat at restaurants more often than those families in which the wife stays home. The fragmented mealtime model has become a way of life for millions of Americans—and in many other cultures, as well.

The following vignette from the experience of an intercultural couple, Gian and Shelly, illustrates how deep-seated our attitudes toward "proper" mealtime manners can be. The couple sat glued to the screen through two showings of Woody Allen's film *Annie Hall*. The movie's depiction of two extremely different family mealtimes reflected the habits of their own families. Gian, a product of a boisterous and spirited Italian family, writes:

> There on the silver screen was Shelly's New England WASP [White Anglo-Saxon Protestant], Daughters of the American Revolution family dinner table. They were so controlled, it was almost unbearable for me to watch. No one ever interrupted anyone else. They carefully picked at the tiny portions of food on their large plates. There was a slight pause between each word. Nothing of any emotional significance was discussed. The gravitational field that held the family together seemed weak, as if any moment everyone might begin to float away from the table and out the windows.
>
> The screen splits in two, and there was Woody Allen's family. They were just like mine when I was growing up. Everyone was crowded around the table,

which was overflowing with food. People bumped elbows as they ate, talked, and interrupted each other. A woman talked about someone's coronary. A husband ate from his wife's plate as she cut his food and yelled at her brother at the same time. If it weren't for the table and the flesh that separated the family members, it seemed like they would all merge together to form a single six-headed being. I knew exactly what it felt like to be at that table.[3]

In the model that Gian describes, neither his nor Shelly's family would be considered "fragmented," yet the two families were complete opposites of each other. Gian's exuberant, well-fed family brings to mind the comment, "The trouble with eating Italian food is that five or six days later you're hungry again!"[4] In contrast, Shelly's reserved family hardly expressed any emotion at all during meals. The dynamics of the two groups differed enormously, creating some difficult conflicts in Gian and Shelly's marriage.

Just like Gian and Shelly, you and your intercultural spouse may hold radically different attitudes about what is considered "acceptable food," "acceptable portions," "acceptable table talk," and "acceptable behavior" during mealtimes. The list of questions provided at the end of this chapter will help you seek to identify your family's cultural patterns and isolate possible problem areas regarding food and mealtimes.

To Eat or Not to Eat . . .

There is not one kind of food for all men. You must and you will feed those faculties which you exercise. The laborer whose body is weary does not require the same food with the scholar whose brain is weary.

—Henry David Thoreau

In some cultures, a meal is not a meal without one or more "staples": tea, rice, noodles, fresh bread, borscht or another type of soup, wine, beans, meat, or potatoes. Hot tea remains such a vital part of the Chinese culture that one of their proverbs asserts: "Better to be deprived of food for three days than tea for one."[5]

Most cultures, countries, and regions enjoy local foods and delicacies particular to that region. For instance, the northern region of Romania where my husband's family lives, called Moldova (not to be confused with the *country* of Moldova, located east of Romania), is famous for its scrumptious soups. My mother-in-law, Maria, makes some of the best, including *ciorba de borta de poi* (a delicious cream-based chicken soup), tripe soup, and "satellite" soup.

Below is a list of countries and some of the traditional foods or regional delicacies that their inhabitants enjoy:

- Australia: Beets on a burger; Morton Bay Bugs (crustaceans similar to crayfish); vegemite (a dark brown, salty food paste made from yeast extract)

- China: Bird's nest soup; jellyfish; owl soup

- Denmark and Iceland: Sild (salted pickled herring)

- England and Ireland: Brawn (head cheese); fish and chips

- France: Calf's head; escargot (snails)

- Germany: Blood sausage; schmaltz (a spread made from chicken fat that is eaten on bread)

- Iceland: Hákarl (fermented, decomposed shark meat)

- Indonesia: Bats; monkey toes; trasi (a paste of salted, fermented prawns)

- Israel and Europe: Gefilte fish (poached balls of ground fish); matzo

- Italy: Cibreo (rooster's comb); songbirds (roasted and eaten whole)

- Japan: Fugu (blowfish), which contains a toxic organ and kills around 300 people in Japan per year

- Korea: Kimchi (fermented cabbage); sea slugs

- Malaysia: Belachan (dried shrimp paste)
- The Netherlands: Rolmops (a slice of raw herring wrapped around a pickle or cocktail onion)
- Norway: Lutefisk (codfish soaked in lye)
- Philippines: Baalut (a fifteen- or sixteen-day-old fertilized duck or chicken egg that is buried in the ground for a few weeks and then eaten complete with eyes, feathers, and feet)
- Romania: Salmale (traditional meat-and-rice rolls); mamaliga (polenta); tripe soup (made with the lining of a calf's stomach)
- Scotland: Dookers (a type of long-beaked, black and white diving seabird); haggis (spicy sausage mixed with oatmeal and stuffed in sheep's intestines)
- Sweden: Surströmming (fermented herring)
- Tunisia: Roasted sheep's head (complete with brains and eyes)
- United States: Casserole; New York-style cheesecake; Philly cheesesteak; chicken-fried steak; chicken livers; collard, mustard, and turnip greens; crayfish; fried green tomatoes; geoduck clams; marshmallows; peanut butter; po'boy sandwiches; pork chitterlings; Tex-Mex food; turducken (a turkey stuffed with a duck stuffed with a chicken and deep fried)[6]

Spend some time discussing this list with your spouse. Are there any foods on the list that he or she enjoys? What about you? Find out which delicacies are common in your spouse's country. Which sound interesting to you? Are there any that you'd be unwilling to try? (I must admit there are several foods on this list that I can't imagine eating!) If so, be sure to tell your spouse beforehand to avoid an uncomfortable situation later. Whenever possible, strive to make food differences something you can laugh about rather than something that causes conflict. (If you or your spouse enjoy certain delicacies not listed in this chapter, please e-mail me at marla_alupoaicei@yahoo.com and share them.)

You'll also find that habits and attitudes toward drinking water, alcohol, and other beverages vary widely in different cultures. When traveling in Europe, I discovered that I tend to drink much more water than my husband and his family. A friend of mine, Carol, remarked that when she and her husband spent time sightseeing in London, their guide worked nonstop from 9:00 a.m. to 9:00 p.m. and drank very little water the entire day, while the rest of the team grew extremely dehydrated. If you plan to travel overseas, take bottled water with you, and be prepared to purchase water or other drinks for your own consumption when you arrive. Also, in many cultures, ice is a rare luxury, so if you prefer ice in your drinks, take along a couple of inexpensive plastic ice cube trays so you can make ice when you reach your destination.

In many European countries as well as some others, people commonly drink alcoholic beverages with meals. If you were traveling in Germany or France, you might be offered only wine or beer to drink rather than water, tea, or another beverage. Refusing the offer of alcoholic beverages can be a delicate matter. If you do not drink alcohol (as neither my husband nor I do), you may either accept a small glass and not drink out of it, or politely inform your host that you don't drink alcoholic beverages. Most hosts will graciously offer you an alternate choice.

Chestnuts Roasting on an Open Fire . . .

If more of us valued food and cheer and song above hoarded gold, it would be a merrier world.
—J. R. R. Tolkien

In virtually every culture, meals hold enormous spiritual and religious significance. The Bible records numerous feasts designed to help the Israelite people remember God's provision and deliverance in their lives, and Jewish people still commemorate those feasts today. Around the globe, special meals are served to celebrate baptisms and christenings, birthdays, funerals, confirmations, weddings, anniversaries, graduations, and religious holidays.

Holiday meals represent nostalgic affairs laden with particular foods and traditions. You might be surprised to find your husband or wife saying, "Christmas just isn't Christmas without duck à l'orange" or, as my husband told me, "On Easter in Romania, we eat a huge meal of roasted lamb, boiled eggs, and beet salad." Even if you've been married for years, don't assume you know what your spouse finds special for the holidays—ask! Most likely, you'll discover some new foods or traditions that you can incorporate into your family's intercultural celebration.

Most of us have distinct memories of holidays past that involve food. Think of some foods that you associate with particular holidays such as Thanksgiving, Christmas, New Year's Day, or Easter. For example, some of my favorite Thanksgiving foods are

- Roast turkey
- My Grandma Walker's homemade dressing
- Candied sweet potatoes
- Scalloped corn
- Cranberry sauce
- My Aunt Jana's mashed potatoes with cheese
- Homemade dinner rolls
- Pumpkin pie
- My mother's applesauce cake

You can see that some of these foods are particular to my family and its traditions. The same most likely will be the case for you and your spouse. One helpful way that you can remember your spouse's special holidays (and the foods particular to those holidays) is for the two of you to sit down together with a calendar and, beginning with January, have your mate list all of his or her culture's holidays while you write down the dates. Also record the specific foods and traditions associated with each holiday. Then, when you purchase a new calendar each year, mark down these special holidays so you don't forget them. You may also add them to your Palm Pilot, Day timer, Outlook calendar, or other scheduling system.

Food as a Love Language

> Love doesn't just sit there, like a stone; it has to be made, like bread, remade all the time, made new.
> —Ursula K. LeGuin

My research and interviews on the subject of food and culture have led me to the conclusion that many people consider a delicious, well-prepared meal to be one of the most treasured and appreciated expressions of love a person could offer.

We've all heard the saying, "The way to a man's heart is through his stomach"[7]—and, in many cases, that's true. Consider the biblical example of Isaac and Rebekah and their twin sons, Jacob and Esau. Isaac's wife, Rebekah, favored Jacob because he was a cultured man. Isaac favored Esau, the hunter, in part because Esau would prepare wild game for his father to eat. Isaac, who had become blind in his old age, asked Esau to hunt and prepare a savory meal for him before he bestowed his fatherly blessing on him (Genesis 27:2–4).

Rebekah sneakily eavesdropped on the conversation and encouraged Jacob to choose two young goats from the flock so she could make a hearty meal for Isaac. She then told Jacob to put on Esau's clothes and place the skins of the goats over his hands and his neck, because Esau was a hairy man. Jacob did so and took the meat to his father, convincing Isaac to give the blessing to him instead of to Esau, whom he was impersonating. When Esau discovered what had happened, he despaired, saying, "Is he not rightly named Jacob [whose name could mean "deceiver"], for he has supplanted me these two times? He took away my birthright, and behold, now he has taken away my blessing." And he pleaded with his father, asking, "Have you not reserved a blessing for me?" (Genesis 27:36). Isaac did bless Esau, but he could not renounce the greater blessing that he had already bestowed upon Jacob.

Several times in this chapter, we find references to "the food which Isaac loved" (Genesis 27:4, 9, 14). Clearly, food played an important role in his life and even, as we can see, led him to favor the son who hunted and prepared savory food for him. Most likely, food represented a love language for Isaac, and he may have passed that language down to his son Esau.

Early in my marriage, I realized that cooking is a valuable love language to my husband, too. People in his culture tend to schedule activities around meals rather than the other way around. The women enjoy going to the grocery store in the morning to purchase food, and then they spend a great deal of time lovingly preparing it, serving it, and eating it along with their families. Especially in the wintertime, when activity is limited by the cold weather, meals become the focus of the day and represent a vital way to gather together as a family and mark the passing of time. However, such a powerful focus on mealtimes and food may be frustrating to spouses from other cultures who don't anticipate spending so much time, money, and effort in the planning of meals.

Sara, a young flight attendant for Air Canada, married Joachim, a Portuguese industrialist. Before marriage, Sara had assumed that when Joachim was working, she would be free to spend her days as she chose. Joachim, however, expected Sara to prepare an elaborate noon feast for him each day. Sara felt that her entire life was scheduled around this lunchtime intrusion: shopping for the meal, preparing it, eating it, and then cleaning up after it. She resented the fact that her days were no longer free. Joachim, on the other hand, had grown up taking a "siesta" each day and felt offended by what he considered Sara's neglect of her wifely role.[8]

Toward the beginning of our marriage, Catalin and I also faced several meal-related conflicts. He preferred to eat meals (especially dinner) later than I did. In fact, he *had* to eat dinner later (usually around 9:00 or 10:00 p.m.) because he worked during the day and attended classes in the evenings. At first, I struggled with preparing the evening meal because I was not accustomed to cooking and eating a large dinner so late. Not only am I not a "night owl" in general, but usually,

I'm not hungry late in the evening. Another issue arose because Catalin was used to the hot, home-cooked meals that his mother had made for him for lunch and dinner every day. However, especially in the summertime in Dallas, cooking and eating a hot meal was often the last thing I felt like doing!

We resolved these issues by applying the FIX solution (conFess, Investigate, and eXplore) I described in the previous chapter. First, we 'fessed up, communicating our emotions and our frustration to each other. Then we investigated the real root of the problem, which boiled down to simple selfishness: each of us liked our own personal meal routine, and neither of us wanted to change it! Our "body clocks" and "mealtime clocks" were not on the same schedule.

Last, we explored solutions and agreed to adjust our schedules, let go of certain expectations, work harder to meet in the middle, and offer grace to one another. Out of love for Catalin and the knowledge that he appreciated my cooking, I began to cook more often, and he grew more accustomed to eating lighter meals sometimes (and eating earlier in the evening when possible). To his credit, Catalin has cheerfully adjusted his expectations and preferences to fit the American way of doing things. He has adapted to American food and meal schedules, not only at home but at work, school, and at my family members' and friends' homes. He's been extremely gracious and, thanks to him and the success of the FIX solution, we've now established a workable meal schedule.

The British novelist George Meredith wrote, "Kissing don't last: cookery do!"[9] Thankfully, my husband and I offer proof positive that romance and food can coexist. Those entering intercultural marriage (especially Western women marrying a man from another culture) simply need to recognize that cooking likely will constitute a vital part of their day and of their marriage relationship.

If you're a spouse in need of help with recipes, the Internet boasts thousands of Web sites containing excellent ethnic recipes, resources, and supplies for your cooking pleasure. (Please see the list at the end of this chapter.) Keeping meals lively, healthy, delicious, and enjoyable will help keep the spice in your marriage!

Dishing Out the Questions

Sharing food with another human being is an intimate act that should not be indulged in lightly.

—M. F. K. Fisher

The following list of questions will help you and your spouse think through the many issues that surround the planning, preparing, and serving of meals. First, ask these questions regarding the habits of your and your spouse's *families of origin.* Then discuss the questions again with regard to the habits you want to integrate into *your own marriage relationship as a couple.* This checklist will help you and your spouse determine which of your families' eating habits, foods, and attitudes you want to keep in your own marriage and which you prefer to leave in the past.

1. What types of food and drink should be eaten?

2. How should the food and drink be prepared, and how much of it?

3. At which times should meals be served and eaten, and where?

4. Which meal should be the largest or most important of the day?

5. In what manner should we eat our meals? (i.e., formal or informal; eaten while sitting at the table or on the floor; eaten with or without a person's spouse, children, extended family, or household employees eating at the same time)

6. Which utensils (if any) should we use during meals?

7. What constitutes proper behavior during meals?

8. Which foods should we eat (and how should they be prepared) for holidays and religious celebrations?

Be sure to write down your mate's answers about food and mealtime habits, as you'll find this information extremely valuable in the future. Bon appétit!

Useful Food and Cooking Web Sites

Recipes (Including Ethnic Recipes)
- All Recipes, http://allrecipes.com
- Cooking Light, http://www.cookinglight.com
- Cuisines of the World, Free Ethnic Recipes, http://culturalcuisines.com/Recipes/recipes.html
- The Food Network, http://www.foodtv.com
- Home and Family Network, "Ethnic Recipes," http://www.homeandfamilynetwork.com/food/ ethnic.html
- Recipe Goldmine, http://www.recipegoldmine.com
- The Recipe Link, "Ethnic and Regional Cooking," http://www.recipelink.com/rcpeth.html
- The Recipe Portal, http://www.therecipeportal.com
- Recipe Source, http://www.recipesource.com/ethnic

Ethnic Cooking Supplies and Utensils
- Cooking.com, http://www.cooking.com
- Cooks Corner, "Ethnic Cooking," http://www.cookscorner.com
- Kitchen Etc., http://www.kitchenetc.com

QUOTE *for reflection*

Come, all you who are thirsty,
come to the waters;
and you who have no money,
come, buy and eat!
Come, buy wine and milk
without money and without cost.
Why spend money on what is not bread,
and your labor on what does not satisfy?
Listen, listen to me, and eat what is good,
and your soul will delight in the richest of fare.

●Isaiah 55:1–2 NIV

MOVIES *to watch*

Annie Hall
**starring Woody Allen
and Diane Keaton
(1977, Rated PG)**

Babette's Feast
**starring Stéphane Audran
and Jean-Philippe Lafont
(1987, Rated G)**

Chocolat
**starring Juliette Binoche
and Johnny Depp
(2000, Rated PG-13)**

9 [MANAGING YOUR FINANCES]

IF YOU MAKE money your god, it will plague you like the devil.

[Henry Fielding[1]]

Bob came running into the house and called out, "Honey! Look at the new DVD player I bought!" His wife, Sarah, exited the kitchen and entered the living room with a frown on her face.

As Bob anxiously opened the DVD player and described all its features, Sarah became more and more aggravated. "We don't have money to be buying DVD players," she said.

"Of course we do! We're getting our tax refund soon. Plus, it was on sale. I've wanted one of these for so long. When I saw it in the electronics store, I just couldn't wait to buy it."

"We were supposed to save our tax refund toward a down payment on a house!"

"There's no way we're ever going to have enough money for a down payment. So why not enjoy the money now? Plus, think of all the movies we can watch together."

Sarah became flooded with emotion and yelled at Bob, "How could you be so selfish!"

"Me?! Selfish?! I bought this DVD player for both of us! Why are you always such a tightwad?"[2]

This scenario occurs over and over in households world-wide. Often, a "spender" like Bob marries a "saver" like Sarah, and conflict ensues. Marriage counselors list "arguments about money" as the number one stated cause of divorce in America. But it's important for us to remember that money itself is neutral; it's *the love of money* (and poor management of money) that gets us into trouble!

One author points out,

> Contrary to a widespread misquotation, the Bible says that *the love of money* (not money itself) is a root of *all kinds of* evil. . . . Money itself is morally neutral, a medium for the exchange of goods and services. But human beings are evil, and their hunger for money is itself evil and is also a cause of other kinds of evil. Strictly speaking, money is an innocent party, so to speak. But human beings are not innocent. In sixteenth-century reformer John Calvin's words, our hearts are "idol factories." It is precisely because the love of money is such a terrible problem for people like us that the Bible has so much to say about the proper attitude toward money. Because our hearts are sinful, God forbids us to love, desire, or run after riches (1 Timothy 6:9–11; Proverbs 23:4–5; Hebrews 13:5).[3]

To avoid serious conflicts regarding finances, every Christian intercultural couple must develop a balanced budget that honors God and reflects the couple's priorities. Couples should also ask each other questions and communicate openly about important financial issues, including:

- budgeting
- tithing
- planning for large purchases (cars, homes, trips, vacations)
- financial planning
- saving
- retirement planning
- purchasing life insurance
- making a will
- naming beneficiaries
- appointing guardians for children

• providing financial support for one or both spouse's
families

Discussing these issues in the marriage-planning stages (or
early in the marriage) and continuing to communicate about
budgeting and spending will help intercultural couples avoid
heated conflict over finances. An excellent starting point for
those who need to establish a budget and learn about financial
planning is to purchase Howard Dayton's book *Your Money
Map* and consider the other products and services provided by
Crown Financial Ministries. For information about Crown Financial Ministries and to contact a financial coach or find out
about seminars in your area, see www.crown.org or call 1 (800)
722-1976.

Cultures and Finances

Earning money to support the family (and deciding how
that money is spent) has traditionally been a male role. In many
cultures of the world, this is still the case. In other cultures
women work to support the family and may even be the primary breadwinners. Many women enjoy contributing to the financial well-being of their families by working. They also gain
satisfaction from having a job and being able to interact with
people outside the home.

In some cultures, men may take on part or all of the home
and child care responsibilities to help support their working
wives. In others, the woman may be expected to stay home full
time to care for the home and children. In some partnerships,
the woman may be expected to work part time or full time and
still cook, clean, and care for the children at home. The attitudes and traditions of each individual's culture will greatly
determine how financial responsibilities and roles are determined in an intercultural marriage.

The following true story provides an illustration.

Lee is an African-American woman; her mother-in-law,
Marcy, is of Jewish ancestry. A few years ago, Lee realized that some of the tension between them had to do

with a cultural misunderstanding related to finances. Marcy felt her daughter-in-law, a hairstylist, had treated her contemptuously. Her annoyance was connected to times when she and her husband were in Atlanta, and Lee had packed a picnic lunch for them to take on the drive back to Connecticut. Not surprising, Lee was baffled: How could anyone misconstrue the meaning behind a carefully prepared picnic? Marcy, on the other hand, thought Lee was suggesting that she was too cheap to stop at a restaurant for lunch. Lee didn't understand Marcy's assumption.

One day, however, Lee read a story about an African-American woman who explained that whenever she went on a trip, she brought a picnic lunch. She said that even when her daughter, the chair of a department at a major university, visited, she insisted that her daughter allow her to "pack her a lunch." This woman added that although she knew the food was completely unnecessary, she could recall days when she couldn't stop at a restaurant because of segregation policies. She concluded, "A lot of us have forgotten why we offer the food to others. It's like saying, 'I hope your trip goes smoothly.' It's the black version of bon voyage."

Now that Lee had a cultural understanding of her own motives, she wondered whether there was an explanation for Marcy's reaction. The next time they were together, Lee blurted out what she had learned. Marcy was touched, and told Lee that when she was a child, kids had teased her about being Jewish. "They said Jews were cheap, and that Daddy slept on a mattress stuffed with money. This was during the Depression when people were suffering. I was critical of you because I was trying to get back at those kids. I'm sorry." The conversation marked a turning point in their relationship.[4]

Author Dugan Romano describes an intercultural couple who faced financial conflict.

Mario did everything he could to sabotage Deirdre's attempts to pick up the career she had left when she married and followed him to Italy. "The evils of the world stem from the woman who works," he told her, implying that she would inevitably fail in her true role as wife and mother if she did less than devote herself exclusively to home and family. He also always managed to minimize the importance of her work; as far as he was concerned, it could be interrupted or put aside if he had a more pressing "need" for her attention. This really upset her, but because the income her work brought in was modest, she was never able to convince him that her career was important.[5]

Author Joel Crohn writes,

I spoke to one young woman from a white Protestant background whose parents were extremely upset when she began to date a Chinese-American man who worked as a landscaper. The young woman said, "My parents worked hard to talk me out of my relationship. They never talked about his income, which wasn't great, but kept on focusing on the problems they claimed that most interracial couples had. They cited some statistics they had read somewhere about the incredibly high divorce rates of interracial couples. Two years later, after Bob and I broke up, I started going out with Alan, who happens to be Japanese-American and who also happens to be a physician. Suddenly my parents' racial concerns were forgotten. I never confronted them about their change of heart. It was weird. I always assumed that they were kind of racist, but now I realize that what they really are is classist."[6]

Each individual entering a marriage will bring his or her own attitudes about money, spending, debt, and managing finances. In addition, that person will reflect his or her family's and culture's attitudes about financial matters, whether he or she realizes it or not. Getting to the bottom of these attitudes and motivations can be tricky. Love, grace, forgiveness, and prayer are required! The best way to avoid financial conflicts is for each individual to sort out the reasons for his or her attitudes and actions about money, and also for couples to discuss finances at a time when emotions are at an even level. When individuals are angry, sad, frustrated, or bewildered by each other's spending habits or other financial choices, heated arguments tend to follow.

What the Bible Says about Money

We can tell our values by looking at our checkbook stubs.
—Gloria Steinem[7]

You might be surprised at how many principles about money we find in the Bible. Scripture provides us with a solid framework for understanding how to manage, give, save, and spend our money. One author writes,

> Scholars point out that Jesus discusses money more than heaven and hell combined, or that Jesus talked more about money than anyone else in the Bible. Financial teacher Howard Dayton, for example, has counted 2,350 verses in God's word that deal with money. Pastor Rick Warren suggests that stewardship and redemption are the two themes which encompass the whole of Scripture, from Genesis to Revelation. Author John Ortberg asks his readers to ponder why the Bible's Author and Editor would devote twice as many verses to money than to faith and prayer. Such comments remind us how much God has to say about money; they also show us how critical it is for us to pay attention to what God's word says about our possessions and pocketbooks.[8]

Below are just some of the biblical passages dealing with this crucial topic.

He who loves money will not be satisfied with money,
nor he who loves abundance with its income. This too is
vanity. (Ecclesiastes 5:10)

Why do you spend money for what is not bread,
And your wages for what does not satisfy?
Listen carefully to Me, and eat what is good,
And delight yourself in abundance. (Isaiah 55:2)

Better is a little with the fear of the Lord
Than great treasure and turmoil with it. (Proverbs 15:16)

The acquisition of treasures by a lying tongue
Is a fleeting vapor, the pursuit of death. (Proverbs 21:6)

Jesus said, "Do not store up for yourselves treasures on
earth, where moth and rust destroy, and where thieves
break in and steal. But store up for yourselves treasures
in heaven, where neither moth nor rust destroys, and
where thieves do not break in or steal; for where your
treasure is, there your heart will be also. The eye is the
lamp of the body; so then if your eye is clear, your whole
body will be full of light. But if your eye is bad, your
whole body will be full of darkness. If then the light that
is in you is darkness, how great is the darkness! No one
can serve two masters; for either he will hate the one and
love the other, or he will be devoted to one and despise
the other. You cannot serve God and wealth."
(Matthew 6:19–24)

These twelve Jesus sent out after instructing them: "Do
not go in the way of the Gentiles, and do not enter any

city of the Samaritans; but rather go to the lost sheep of the house of Israel. And as you go, preach, saying, 'The kingdom of heaven is at hand.' Heal the sick, raise the dead, cleanse the lepers, cast out demons. Freely you received, freely give. Do not acquire gold, or silver, or copper for your money belts, or a bag for your journey, or even two coats, or sandals, or a staff; for the worker is worthy of his support. " (Matthew 10:5–10)

Jesus said to him, "If you wish to be complete, go and sell your possessions and give to the poor, and you will have treasure in heaven; and come, follow Me." (Matthew 19:21)

And He sat down opposite the treasury, and began observing how the people were putting money into the treasury; and many rich people were putting in large sums. A poor widow came and put in two small copper coins, which amount to a cent. Calling His disciples to Him, He said to them, "Truly I say to you, this poor widow put in more than all the contributors to the treasury; for they all put in out of their surplus, but she, out of her poverty, put in all she owned, all she had to live on. " (Mark 12:41–44)

For the love of money is a root of all sorts of evil, and some by longing for it have wandered away from the faith and pierced themselves with many griefs. (1 Timothy 6:10)

Spend some time reading through these passages and praying with your fiancé or spouse about your finances. What principles from Scripture do you need to apply to your spiritual life and your personal financial priorities? What changes do you and your fiancé or spouse need to make to your saving, spending, and giving habits?

Excellent Resources for Budgeting and Managing Finances

When Catalin and I first married, I worked full time as a writer for a ministry. He began school and also worked part-time. Finances were somewhat tight for us during that time, but we were able to manage well. I wanted him to have the opportunity to pursue his dream of going to college and getting a good job in his field. After Catalin graduated and we both started working full time, our financial situation improved. But we discovered that having more money doesn't always mean that a couple is managing their money in a wiser way. We weren't extravagant with our spending, but if we wanted to buy something (within reason), we typically just bought it without worrying about it too much.

However, in 2006, I began working from home full time as an author, which has been my dream for many years. This required a financial sacrifice for both of us. I enjoyed it very much, but the income that authors receive is not as consistent as the income received from a regular 9 to 5 job. Eventually, it seemed that in order for us to reach our goals of purchasing a home and starting a family, I would need to go back to work part-time. Though that was an extremely difficult decision for me to make, it provided us with the funds to purchase our new home and offered us greater financial stability before our first child was born.

Each couple will need to discuss their goals and make determinations, like we did, of their priorities and of what sacrifices need to be made in order to achieve those priorities. With most couples, one spouse is a spender and the other is a saver. In addition, some cultures (like American culture) tend to emphasize wealth and spending and minimize the consequences of accruing debt. Other cultures emphasize relationships over material things and consider debt to be shameful. Spend some time sharing your family's and your culture's attitudes toward budgeting, spending, saving, wealth, debt, and money management with your fiancé or spouse.

I also recommend the following Christian resources for couples seeking to create a workable budget and manage their finances well:

- *The Total Money Makeover* by Dave Ramsey
- *The Treasure Principle* by Randy Alcorn
- *Your Money Map* by Howard Dayton

QUOTE *for reflection*

Make sure that your character is free from the love of money, being content with what you have; for He Himself has said, "I will never desert you, nor will I ever forsake you."

●Hebrews 13:5

MOVIES *to watch*

The Family Man
starring Nicolas Cage
and Tea Leoni
(2000, Rated PG-13)

The Horse Whisperer
starring Robert Redford
and Kristin Scott Thomas
(1998, Rated PG-13)

10 [Rearing Your Children]

MAKING THE DECISION to have a child—it's momentous. It is to decide forever to have your heart go walking outside your body.

[ELIZABETH STONE[1]]

Once their first child arrives, an intercultural couple's relational dynamics often change radically. I've heard many couples say, "Everything in our marriage was smooth sailing until our first baby was born!" When a child is born, painful conflicts can occur due to the unexpected and confusing mix of emotions and attitudes bubbling to the surface. The enormous responsibility that accompanies the task of child rearing adds an additional burden of stress that can cause a great deal of tension and uncertainty in intercultural marriage.

Because cultural ideas about rearing children are so deeply ingrained, individuals often struggle to identify their own values and attitudes on the topic. Dugan Romano writes,

> Parents who clash over child-rearing issues are often really battling over some basic difference in philosophy, values or beliefs that they as a couple have not managed to resolve. The more emotional and seemingly illogical the reaction to some event or issue, the greater the probability that the cause lies deep within—the child merely provides the spark for conflict. But these underlying issues are often difficult to recognize or define, let alone come to grips with; so, instead of going to the heart of the matter, the couple fights over the particulars.[2]

In most cases, differences of opinion about child care and parenting arise even before an intercultural couple's first child is born. Questions such as these below may surface. If you have not yet discussed these questions openly with your fiancé or spouse, make it a point to sit down with him or her as soon as possible to ask them.

- Do you want to have children at all? If so, how many?

- Are you open to infertility treatments or adoption if we are not able to have children for some reason?

- What religious beliefs and values should we teach our child?

- What church should we attend? Are adequate nursery facilities and children's programs available?

- What type of name will we select?

- Will we raise our child to be monocultural or bicultural? If bicultural, how will we do this? Will it be primarily one spouse's responsibility, or the responsibility of both?

- When and how will we decorate the nursery? Or will the baby stay in the same room with us?

- What language(s) will our child speak? Who will teach these languages to the child?

- Will the wife work outside the home, or will she stay home full time to care for the baby?

- What type of child care responsibilities will the husband have? Will he help feed the baby, change diapers, shop, clean the house, and assist with other chores?

- Will we hire a nanny, housekeeper, language instructor, or other help after the child is born?

- Which family members (if any) will come to help when the child is born? How long will they stay? What boundaries will we set for them as far as accepting child care and advice are concerned? If a conflict arises, who will handle it, and how?

- What customs (such as christening, baptism, dedication, circumcision, or other traditional or religious rituals) does each individual or family typically do before and after the birth of a child? Is your spouse expecting to have these customs performed on the child?

- Are the grandparents and other family members prepared to accept a biracial, bicultural, and bilingual child? Do they understand that the child may not look like their side of the family?

- Do you and/or your spouse plan to ask your family members to support you and help you teach your family's faith, values, customs, and language(s) to your children?

If possible, you'll want to find out the answers to these questions from your partner before getting engaged, and certainly before getting married. Sometimes individuals assume that their spouse wants to have children when he or she actually does not. In other situations, one spouse's assumptions about male and female roles, work, child care, and household responsibilities can come as a shock to a spouse who holds sharply contrasting ideas about these issues. Because having and raising children is one of the most important and life-changing experiences that couples face in their marriages, it's vital that husbands and wives ask questions ahead of time and work hard to achieve harmony in this area.

Intercultural Child Rearing

In Romania and other countries where couples live in apartments or small homes, few couples have enough room to create a separate nursery just for the baby. Most babies sleep in the same bed with their parents. This pattern often continues until the child is much older. In contrast, most American and

Western couples prepare a separate nursery for the baby to sleep in. In my own family, babies and children did not sleep with their parents unless the child was ill or some type of emergency had occurred. Catalin and I recently purchased a new home with a room dedicated for our baby's nursery. We plan to purchase a crib where the baby will sleep.

In addition, many cultures believe in swaddling babies by wrapping them tightly in clothing or fabric strips. They also may believe in keeping the baby in a very warm room, without a fan or open windows. People in these cultures feel that a breeze or draft is harmful for babies and can make them sick.

Also, some cultures believe that it's healthy for babies to be "fattened up." In these cultures, babies are overfed; they may be breast-fed every time they cry. In other cultures, such as in many Western countries, babies are often placed on a feeding schedule. They are fed only at certain intervals in order to regulate their eating and sleeping habits and allow the parents to create a manageable sleeping schedule.

My husband, Catalin, works for a company based in Israel, and many of his colleagues are Jewish. He recently attended a baby shower for a non-Jewish colleague at which the expectant father was discussing how the nursery had already been decorated for the baby's arrival, the baby's name had been chosen, and many preparations for the baby's arrival had already been made. The Jewish employees were very surprised to hear this. One woman noted that in Jewish culture, no one buys clothes, furniture, or anything else for the baby until after the birth. To do so is considered bad luck. Be sure to find out what your partner's culture considers appropriate actions to plan for your baby's arrival.

In certain cultures, rather than praising a newborn baby and saying how beautiful it is, friends and relatives actually "insult" the baby in order to keep evil spirits from harming it. They seek to avoid what they call "the evil eye." They believe that if they draw attention to the baby by emphasizing its beauty, evil spirits will envy the baby and cause it harm. They might say, "Look at what a big head he has!" or "She has such a red face" or "Too bad he has those squinty eyes." A mother and father who are unaccustomed to this type of comment could be extremely offended to hear such remarks about their darling newborn baby! Ask your fiancé or spouse whether or not his or her family and culture believe in making comments like these to avoid "the evil eye."

Author Terri Knudsen profoundly describes her experience of raising her children on foreign soil. She writes,

> I'm an American; my husband is a Dane. The first years of our relationship were spent on "neutral" ground—in South America, where I was teaching and my husband was working for a Danish firm. We lived in three different countries before moving to Denmark. . . . I was suddenly in my husband's country, surrounded by his family and friends, language and culture. I felt very dependent on him and developed an even closer relationship to our children because they were also foreigners in Denmark.
>
> After a short time, my children became "Danes." Instead of English, Danish became the language they felt most comfortable speaking. . . . I find it more and more difficult to hold on to my identity. I feel like a different person depending on the situation I'm in. Danes expect me to be "Danish," because I look like them and have lived here so many years—a Dane with an accent. Americans expect me still to be "American" and don't understand the changes one goes through living abroad. . . .
>
> I am trying to raise my sons in a bilingual and bicultural home. It sounds good in theory, however, in practice it has been one of those experiences I hope I can look back on in years to come and be able to laugh! The result of my efforts is that suddenly I found myself to be the foreigner in our family. I am Lars and Bo's American mother, my husband's American wife, and the American on the block. I have had to learn to accept that my children are now Danes, and they have also reminded me of this from time to time. I'll never forget the day my youngest son turned to me when we were discussing vacation plans and said, "We should decide because we're all

Danes and you're an American. It's three against one!" . . .
During a language course four years ago, we had to draw
a picture of our families. My family was in a circle and I
was on the outside looking in."[3]

Later in her essay, Knudsen notes the ways in which she has
incorporated her own American culture and values into her family. She writes, "I have made sure, for my benefit as well as theirs,
that my children also become a bit 'Americanized.' . . . I have
taught my children 'The Itsy-Bitsy Spider,' read Dr. Seuss to them
and played softball with them. We celebrate Thanksgiving, the
4th of July and Christmas. . . . [My husband and I] have a good
life together and two well-adjusted, happy children."[4]

Susan Perry married a man named John from Lebanon. She
describes the differences between her child-rearing strategies
and those of her mother-in-law, Maryam:

> I thought I knew just about all there was to know about
> [John's] culture until his mother spent four months in
> our house. . . . Many of our conflicts revolved around
> childcare.
>
> Maryam reared eight children to adulthood in a vil-
> lage of three thousand people in the hills of North
> Lebanon. One son had ten children, a daughter had
> twelve, and Maryam helped out often with her grandchil-
> dren. Maybe she did have a right to believe she knew
> more than I did about childrearing. After all, I was an
> only child who had rarely baby-sat, and I got most of my
> parenting knowledge from books and magazines.
>
> [Our son] Simon had begun walking the month be-
> fore Maryam arrived . . . he was running, climbing up,
> and jumping down all day long. Yet wherever he
> zoomed, there was Maryam, chasing after him with her
> arms outstretched, ready to catch him and protect him
> from calamity. She was aghast that I allowed him to play
> in the dirt.
>
> I wanted him to feel free; she wanted him to be
> safe. . . . She thought I was a careless mother. Yet I was

struggling with my own urge to overprotect. I wanted Simon to grow up independent and unafraid—unlike me, who went through childhood plagued by fears. Try explaining that in a foreign language! I couldn't.

When Simon was ill with a stubborn fever and ear infection, and seven visits to the doctor and much medication failed to cure him, Maryam took matters into her own hands. Without a word of explanation, she set about gathering some unexpected items. While I watched, increasingly horrified, she snipped a lock of his hair, tore a few threads from one of his old shirts, clipped one of his fingernails, and set the whole collection on fire in a tuna fish can. She walked around him several times, muttering some words. I was worried she might do something dangerous. Her incantation complete, she put out the fire, leaving me wondering and more than a little annoyed. The next day Simon's fever broke. To me, Maryam's smugness was a wordless "I told you so."[5]

Stories like these provide a reminder of why couples should discuss parenting principles *before* their first child is born and *before* family members come to help care for the child. The sooner a couple can create positive boundaries, the better. Each couple must decide which elements of culture and tradition to incorporate into their personal parenting strategies and which to leave out, and the in-laws, grandparents, and other family members must respect those wishes or conflict will ensue. As when tackling any tough issue, keeping a gracious and forgiving spirit will help couples address issues in a positive manner.

Biblical Principles for Positive Parenting

Anne Frank wrote, "Parents can only give good advice or put [their children] on the right paths, but the final forming of a person's character lies in their own hands."[6] In the early years, parents help to form godly character in their children so that later, children will have a framework for making wise decisions on their own. I've been blessed to have wonderful, godly parents who love and serve the Lord and who taught us to do

the same. My mother, Dorothy Martin, has these parenting
principles to share:

Discipline—The biblical concepts of parental discipline
are the same, no matter what the culture. A child *has* to
learn to obey his parents. The sinful human nature manifests itself early on in a child's life, with emphasis on
"me" and "mine." A parent has to teach a child to share
and to speak kind words. Sometimes it takes a lot of patience, but the child must realize that he wants to treat
others the way he would like to be treated. A child has to
learn to obey his parents' voice and trust his parents'
judgment. Safety and survival can depend on that. Disciplinary measures need to be matter of fact, and carried
out exactly as said. Mom and Dad *have* to be on the same
page when it comes to disciplinary measures. It works
best to write things out so everyone knows what has
been decided, and then follow through with it. A parent
has to have a mind-set of perseverance when it comes to
discipline. The words *I mean business* can be effective. For
instance, if a child is arguing with a parent, that parent
could say, "I said 'No,' and I mean business." This can be
said in a matter-of-fact voice with no yelling or arguing. For older children, the concept of "with privilege
comes responsibility" can be helpful. If the child has dis-
obeyed, then privileges have to be taken away.

Teach Your Child to Have Faith in God—Start with
singing "Jesus Loves Me." A child needs to hear the
names of God and Jesus from the beginning. Pray at a
child's level. Introduce God through nature. Read simple
Bible stories. Help your child memorize brief Scrip-
tures. Start church experiences early—the nursery,
Sunday school class, junior church, and Awana. Be consistent with faith training. Have an open Bible in the
home. Have devotions and pray together every night
before going to sleep.

Help Your Child Become the Person God Desires—
Provide a wide range of activities for your child, and
watch for your child's "bent." Encourage creativity. Spend
time outdoors. As a child becomes older, the child and
parents should pray together for God's wisdom for the
child's life work, and how to prepare for it.

Teach Your Child to Cherish His Heritage—This can be
especially exciting in an intercultural home. Share family
traditions. Make traditional foods. Purchase a globe and
show your children where their ancestors or other family
members came from. Tell family stories, both sad ones
and funny ones. Describe how family members came to
know the Lord. Create a family album or scrapbook, so if
a particular family member is mentioned, you can show
your child a picture of that person.

The following Bible passages offer additional parenting
principles and promises to intercultural couples.

> *"I have no greater joy than this, to hear of my children
> walking in the truth."* (3 John 1:4)

> *"You shall love the Lord your God with all your heart and
> with all your soul and with all your might. These words,
> which I am commanding you today, shall be on your
> heart. You shall teach them diligently to your sons and
> shall talk of them when you sit in your house and when
> you walk by the way and when you lie down and when
> you rise up. . . . You shall not follow other gods. . . . You
> shall not put the Lord your God to the test. . . . You
> should diligently keep the commandments of the Lord
> your God, and His testimonies and His statutes which
> He has commanded you. You shall do what is right and
> good in the sight of the Lord, that it may be well with
> you."* (Deuteronomy 6:5–18)

"Just as a father has compassion on his children,
So the Lord has compassion on those who fear Him."
(Psalm 103:13)

"Behold, children are a gift of the Lord,
The fruit of the womb is a reward.
Like arrows in the hand of a warrior,
So are the children of one's youth.
How blessed is the man whose quiver is full of them;
They will not be ashamed
When they speak with their enemies in the gate."
(Psalm 127:3–5)

"Children, obey your parents in the Lord, for this is
right." (Ephesians 6:1)

"Fathers, do not exasperate your children, so that they
will not lose heart." (Colossians 3:21)

Excellent Childrearing and Parenting Resources

George Santayana said, "A child educated only at school is an uneducated child."[7] Parents bear the primary responsibility for raising a healthy, happy child with positive character qualities and biblical values. They also are responsible to teach their child that God loves him or her and that he or she needs to establish a personal relationship with Christ. The following books (most of which are Christian books) will provide a solid foundation for parents:

- *Babyproofing Your Marriage* by Stacie Cockrell, Cathy O'Neill, and Julia Stone
- *The Five Love Languages of Children* by Gary Chapman and Ross Campbell
- *Grace-Based Parenting* by Tim Kimmel
- *The Happiest Baby on the Block* by Harvey Karp

- *Have a New Kid by Friday* by Kevin Leman
- *The New Strong-Willed Child* by Dr. James Dobson
- *Parenting from the Inside Out* by Daniel Siegel and Mary Hartzell
- *Parenting Today's Adolescent* by Dennis Rainey
- *Parenting with Love and Logic* by Foster Cline and Jim Fay
- *Playful Parenting* by Lawrence Cohen
- *The Power of a Praying Parent* by Stormie Omartian
- *Secrets of the Baby Whisperer* by Tracy Hogg and Melinda Blau
- *Shepherding a Child's Heart* by Tedd Tripp
- *What the Bible Says about Parenting* by John MacArthur

For additional parenting assistance, contact your local church to see if they operate a Mother's Day Out program, Bible studies for parents, or other parenting support groups. Many communities also offer Mothers of Preschoolers (MOPS) groups. For more information about MOPS groups in your area, see www.mops.org or call toll-free at 1 (888) 910-MOPS.

To get information about support groups for children with special needs and their families, contact Joni and Friends Disability Ministry at 1 (818) 707-5664.

QUOTE *for reflection*

Train up a child in the way he should go,
Even when he is old he will not depart from it.
●Proverbs 22:6

MOVIES *to watch*

Empire of the Sun
starring Christian Bale
and John Malkovich
(1987, Rated PG)

Life Is Beautiful
starring Roberto Benigni, Nicoletta Braschi,
and Giorgio Cantarini
(1997, Rated PG-13)

Not Without My Daughter
starring Sally Field
and Alfred Molina (1991, Rated PG-13)

11 [Dealing
with Illness
and Grief]

EARTH HAS NO sorrow that heaven cannot heal.

[Author Unknown¹]

llness, grief, and loss are part of the human experience, yet attitudes about them vary from culture to culture. In one intercultural study on illness, McGoldrick, Giordano, and Pearce state that people across cultures differ in the following ways:

1. How they experience pain

2. What they label as a symptom

3. How they communicate their pain or symptoms

4. What their beliefs are about the cause of illness

5. How they regard medical professionals (doctors and therapists)

6. What treatment they desire or expect[2]

Before marrying, intercultural couples should ask each other about their individual and cultural attitudes toward illness, suffering, and grief. Later on in this chapter, you'll find a list of questions to help you.

I've encountered several differences in attitudes on these topics between Romanian culture and American culture. Many of these apply in other marriages with an Eastern/Western dynamic. In Eastern cultures, many people believe that the air outside (especially the night air) is unhealthy and can cause illness. In contrast, in Western cultures, people tend to believe that breathing fresh air is healthy. I enjoy walking and running outside, and I often open windows in our home and in the car in order to get the air moving. I also like to sleep with the fan on. In addition, in Texas, using the air conditioner is non-negotiable for at least eight months out of the year. Personally, I start to feel ill if I am in a stuffy room, in a hot vehicle, or on a train without any moving air. But my husband's family doesn't enjoy having windows open or fans on, so when I am visiting there, I have to adjust my expectations. They believe that they will become ill if they are exposed to moving air. Also, their ideas sometimes become self-fulfilling prophecy: if they do get a cold, they blame it on a time when they were exposed to the night air or were sitting by a fan.

I also have found myself a bit hesitant to accept medical advice or treatment when traveling in Romania. To be honest, I considered the medical system there to be inferior and I didn't want to take medicine that I was unfamiliar with. In May 2008, Catalin and I traveled to Romania for his sister Andreea's wedding. While there, I caught a cold—sniffles, runny nose, achy head, sore throat, the works. I needed medicine, but I was concerned about taking something that I was unsure of. We stopped by a little pharmacy where the pharmacist recommended that I take medicine called Coldrex, which contained paracetamol. I had never heard of paracetamol, and I have to admit that I was very apprehensive, assuming that Romanian medicine would not work as well as the kind I typically take in the States. In addition, I feared that I might have some strange reaction or side effects from taking it.

The instructions said that I should take a packet of the Coldrex and stir it into a tall glass of hot water. We went to the mall in Cluj, where a new Starbucks had just opened, and we asked for a cup of hot water. The girl gave me a tiny wax cup of water that was about half the size of a Dixie cup. I stirred the Coldrex packet into it and took a sip. The hot, bitter, lemony stuff was the most disgusting thing I have ever tasted in my life. I shuddered as I kept taking tiny sips of it. *This can't possibly be working*, I thought. Somehow, I managed to down most of the concoction. *If only I had my trusty Advil Cold and Sinus*, I moaned to myself.

But the next morning I woke up and I was completely well. No sniffles. No runny nose. No achy head. No sore throat. I learned my lesson about European medicine: that stuff works! It may not taste good, but it does the job. I had to repent of my previously held notions about medical treatment in Romania.

Several years ago, my husband discovered that Cristi, one of his best friends from high school, had passed away from cancer in Romania. Adding to the pain of that loss was the fact that Cristi had been gone for at least a month before Catalin found out about his death, so there was no time for my husband to make travel arrangements to attend the funeral. The fact that Catalin could not be there for Cristi and his family during this sad time, plus the knowledge that he could not go back to pay his respects and to reminisce about old times with all of his high school friends, was a great loss for Catalin. In addition, the loss of a close friend forced my husband and his friends, at a very young age, to come face-to-face with their own mortality.

I asked Catalin to share some differences between the grieving/mourning process in Romania and the process here. He listed the following:

- Grief is more public in Romania. It seems to be more private and personal in the States.

- People in Romania are more inclined to show their grief externally with crying and mourning.

- In some of the villages in Romania, the men don't shave for forty days after a loved one dies.

- The funeral procession (with the body in an open casket) is led through the streets so people are able to participate in the grieving process with the family.

- Leaflets with obituary and funeral information typically are posted throughout the city or village. Most people don't read the newspapers, so this assures that everyone in the city knows about the person's passing and when the funeral will be held.

- In the Orthodox tradition, young men who pass away before they have the opportunity to get married usually are dressed in a wedding suit, and young women in the same case are dressed in a wedding dress for their burial.

As I've observed and studied the responses to death across a broad spectrum of cultures, I've concluded that grief, loss, and death in America are extremely sanitized. When I first moved to Dallas, one of the most shocking aspects of the city that I noticed right away was that there were no cemeteries (not that I could see, anyway). Of course, some cemeteries do exist here, but they seem to be hidden away from view so that no one has to think about death. In Illinois and Indiana, where I grew up, I passed cemeteries every day. My older brother, who passed away at the age of four, is buried in a small country cemetery in Atwood, Illinois. Every time I visit my grandparents and other family members there, I'm reminded of him and of the precious and short nature of life on this earth.

In contrast with Western cultures, most cultures consider death to be a natural part of the life cycle, just as winter is a part of the earth's seasonal cycle. People in these cultures accept death, and they expect it. They don't shy away from its scary, painful, and ugly aspects. In fact, they use death and grief as a reason to celebrate life and to spend precious time with family and friends, remembering the blessings of yesterday and today. They honor the process of aging and death instead of trying to eliminate the process altogether.

Managing Grief and Loss

Every married couple will encounter illness, grief, loss, and the death of a loved one at some point in their relationship. Each individual will benefit by examining his or her personal and cultural attitudes toward these painful issues.

Cultures vary widely in their attitudes toward bereavement, and failing to follow a particular culture's rules can have significant consequences. For instance, in most cases in Japan, the burial of bodies is outlawed; bodies must be cremated. This practice fits Japanese culture and religious beliefs, but may be offensive to a person from another culture who does not wish for his or her loved one to be cremated. Most Western cultures (especially Christian ones) have an elevated view of the body and prefer burial to cremation.

When Dorrie's Japanese husband, Hiroshi, passed away, Dorrie struggled with making the arrangements for his cremation. Dugan Romano writes, "It was not so much the cremation that she found difficult but the ceremony that followed, when family members transferred the ashes into an urn with chopsticks. She found the whole event emotionally draining and distasteful, but for his family it was an important part of saying good-bye."[3]

Some people are surprised at how grief makes them want to return to their cultural roots or their homeland. Alex, a Japanese-American man, writes:

> "When I started dating Ashley, who is from a WASP background, I acted like being Japanese was of no real significance to me. We never talked about our different backgrounds. But when my mother became ill and died last year, I was shocked by my own feelings—I suddenly started to feel Japanese for the first time in my life. I couldn't believe that I felt guilty about bringing Ashley to the funeral because she was white. I made up excuses to explain why I wanted to go to the funeral alone, and Ashley got very upset and asked me if I was ashamed of being with her."[4]

The Five Stages of Grief

Dr. Elisabeth Kübler-Ross has engaged in decades of groundbreaking research in the field of death and dying. In her book *On Death and Dying*, first published in 1969, Dr. Kübler-Ross lists the five stages of the grieving process (which can apply to any significant loss) as follows:

- **Denial**—This stage involves thoughts like, "It can't be true! I feel fine. The doctors must have made a mistake" or "That person can't really be gone."

- **Anger**—This stage involves emotions like, "Why me, God? It's so unfair."

- **Bargaining**—This stage involves bargaining and praying for more time, as in, "Please let me live to see my children get married" or, "If You heal me, I'll devote the rest of my life to doing _____."

- **Depression**—This stage involves deep emotions of despair and depression as the reality of the grief or disease sets in. A person might think, "Why bother to get out of bed in the morning?" or "Why even try to fight this disease? I'm going to die anyway, so what's the point?"

- **Acceptance**—This final stage involves acceptance and usually a more balanced and healthy view of a person's disease or situation. The person recognizes his or her situation and tries to make the best of it. He or she may realize that fighting the disease is the only way to live longer, or that accepting the grief of a loss and moving on is the only way to find healing.[5]

Grief is intensely personal, so naturally its nuances will be far more complex than this list can communicate. In addition, the emotions that accompany grief (as well as what is considered the *acceptable manner* of expressing those emotions) may vary from culture to culture. This list of stages simply provides a helpful basic framework for understanding grief and loss. Not all people will show evidence of passing through all of these stages when grieving. However, being aware of these grief steps will help couples to empathize with each other and to better cope when helping each other face a difficult illness, death, or other unexpected loss.

A licensed Christian counselor also can help tremendously in enabling grieving individuals to move through these five stages in a healthy way. If you and your spouse are facing grief and loss that seems overwhelming, please talk with your pastor or a counselor.

Over the seven years of our marriage, Catalin and I have faced a variety of experiences that have caused us grief and stress. A young man from our couples' class at church announced that his wife left him and wants a divorce. We recently chose not to purchase two homes that we had placed offers on, and lost money on both. We found out that a good friend is unable to have children, and another friend had a miscarriage. We discovered that a pastor friend of ours has an alcohol addiction. In addition, we found out that a close friend's family member was killed in a car accident.

Though we grieved each of these losses, Catalin and I also discovered that they opened up doors of opportunity for ministry that we never would have encountered otherwise. Many other intercultural couples find the same to be true in their marriages. Art, an American whose parents had been missionaries in Korea, married Sue, a South Korean woman. Art says, "The most difficult thing in our life was when, after having two fine healthy boys, our third child, Elaine, was born with physical and mental handicaps. Although Elaine is now sixteen, mentally she is about age three. This situation has been hard for both of us."

Sue adds, "Taking care of Elaine at home for ten years kept me very busy. But, thankfully, through caring for her I was given a sympathy and concern for all handicapped people. Later I was able to develop a ministry to handicapped people in Korea—which is a great need because there is a temptation for some Koreans from a Buddhist background to neglect handicapped children, thinking their problems are a result of 'karma' or a 'punishment' for having done something bad in a previous incarnation. Thankfully, as Christianity grows in Korea, this attitude of seeing handicapped children as a 'shameful burden' is changing and my ministry to the handicapped has been very rewarding."[6]

The Grief of Moving

The experience of moving from one culture to another can also cause deep grief, loss, and frustration for intercultural couples. When a couple first moves away from one or both spouse's home and family, they often experience culture shock. Even after the foreign spouse gets over the initial culture shock, he or she is usually at some disadvantage in the foreign culture and society, and the spouse from that culture will need to be sensitive to those issues—probably for many, many years, if not always. Much of the struggle has to do with language, but other issues may also arise, like dealing with the native government and health care system. Even if an individual eventually moves back to his or her home country after a period of years, that person may experience "reverse culture shock" when he or she discovers that things at home are not as they were years ago.

In their book *In Love But Worlds Apart*, G. Shelling and J. Fraser-Smith write:

> Moving back home sounds like a dream come true at last, but it can be quite a shock to return there. So many things have changed; other things are simply not remembered. The people are not the same: some have grown old, others have moved, and still others do not remember the returnee. New buildings have been built and landmarks have been torn down. Even the music has changed. The partner who is going back to his or her own country is in reverse culture shock.
>
> Helena [from Greece] had studied in Canada and then returned home to Greece. Although she had really looked forward to coming home, she felt at first that she didn't really belong there anymore. Even worse, she felt totally estranged. Some things had changed while she was gone; there were new streets and many new houses. Some of her favorite landmarks were torn down. Even the music had changed on the radio. . . . Commodity products easily bought in Canada had not yet reached Greece. . . . To her surprise, she missed Canada.[7]

In contrast, Helena's husband, Jay, was experiencing culture shock as he moved to Greece for the first time. Shelling and Fraser-Smith describe, "He couldn't understand at all what Helena was going through in her 'reverse culture shock.' He expected her to know everything and be there for him. But because she was still trying to re-adjust, she struggled to be patient. She tried at first, but soon she tired of helping him to learn the language and to adjust to the Greek culture. As she recovered from her reverse culture shock, she was able to help him in his adjustment."[8]

Catalin also faced a bit of culture shock when he arrived in the States. I attended Dallas Theological Seminary in downtown Dallas at that time. One of the first surprises Catalin encountered was seeing homeless people on the street corners downtown, holding signs and begging for food. I suppose he thought that this happened only in the movies, not in real life in the United States of America.

Probably the most difficult adjustment for my husband has been to acclimate to the different way that people interact here in the States, and especially in Dallas. The fast-paced lifestyle allows little time for people to cultivate deep relationships. People tend to be more distant and task-oriented. They don't just stop by our house to chat on their way to the store. Although Catalin speaks English well and has done very well in school and in his jobs, I know he's still disappointed by the fact that the relationships here seem superficial. Most of his best friends are still back in Romania.

Dealing with Stress, Conflict, Illness, and Grief

Individuals manage stress and react to conflict in a variety of ways. Most couples find that when a difference of opinion arises, one partner prefers to stay and fight, while the other prefers to take flight. Intercultural partners should ask each other the following questions:

- When you feel ill, how do you tend to act? Do you go to the doctor immediately, or do you usually try to wait it out?

- When you were growing up, how did your parents treat you when you were ill?

- Are there certain foods and beverages that you prefer to eat and drink when you get sick?

- How do you typically respond to a crisis? Give an example from your childhood or adult life.

- In your family of origin, how did different individuals tend to respond in stressful or crisis situations?

- What are the warning signals that you are getting upset?

- How do you signal that you want to take a time-out from discussing a certain issue?

- When you face stress at home, at work, or within the family, how do you normally handle that stress?

- What is your understanding of biblical ways to resolve conflict in our marriage?

- When you are angry or upset, do you tend to want to talk and argue until the issue is resolved, or do you retreat and give the other person "the silent treatment"?

- What do you think it means to "fight fair"?

- What active measures do you think we can take now to help avoid future conflicts in our marriage?

- What situations in your life have caused you grief? How do you tend to manage your grief?

- In your culture, was death discussed openly and accepted as a natural part of life, or was the topic ignored or treated as taboo? How did your family deal with the topic of death, attending funerals, etc.?

- In your family and culture, was grief openly expressed (by crying, mourning, talking about the loss, or other manifestations) or was grief something that was usually suppressed and not shown?

- In your own marriage and family, what do you consider to be the proper expression of grief?

Many intercultural spouses grow disillusioned when they discover how differently each one responds to a crisis or loss. Every couple should ask each other the questions listed above in order to sort through their personal attitudes about illness, conflict, and grief. This will enable couples to take the first step toward finding workable, biblical ways to manage and minimize conflict in order to develop a joyful, healthy marriage that glorifies God.

Biblical Encouragement for Those Facing Illness, Grief, and Loss

The following Scripture passages offer hope, encouragement, and biblical guidance for those experiencing illness, conflict, grief, and loss:

Therefore you too have grief now; but I will see you again, and your heart will rejoice, and no one will take your joy away from you. (John 16:22)

Is anyone among you sick? Then he must call for the elders of the church and they are to pray over him, anointing him with oil in the name of the Lord; and the prayer offered in faith will restore the one who is sick, and the Lord will raise him up, and if he has committed sins, they will be forgiven him. Therefore, confess your sins to one another, and pray for one another so that you may be healed. The effective prayer of a righteous man can accomplish much. (James 5:14–16)

How blessed is he who considers the helpless;
The Lord will deliver him in a day of trouble.
The Lord will protect him and keep him alive,
And he shall be called blessed upon the earth;
And do not give him over to the desire of his enemies.
The Lord will sustain him upon his sickbed;
In his illness, You restore him to health. (Psalm 41:1–3)

Consider it pure joy, my brothers, whenever you face trials
of many kinds, because you know that the testing of your
faith develops perseverance. Perseverance must finish its
work so that you may be mature and complete, not lack-
ing anything. If any of you lacks wisdom, he should ask
God, who gives generously to all without finding fault,
and it will be given to him. But when he asks, he must be-
lieve and not doubt, because he who doubts is like a wave
of the sea, blown and tossed by the wind. That man
should not think he will receive anything from the Lord;
he is a double-minded man, unstable in all he does.
(James 1:2–8 NIV)

I pray that the principles and questions provided in this chapter will help you and your spouse work through grief and loss throughout the years of your marriage. The following resources will also provide practical encouragement and biblical principles for you:

- *Experiencing Grief* by H. Norman Wright
- *Getting to the Other Side of Grief: Overcoming the Loss of a Spouse* by Susan J. Zonnebelt-Smeenge and Robert C. De Vries
- *Good Grief* by Granger E. Westberg
- *When Grief Comes* by Kirk H. Neely

QUOTES *for reflection*

My soul weeps because of grief;
Strengthen me according to Your word.
● Psalm 119:28

Weeping may last for the night,
But a shout of joy comes in the morning.
● Psalm 30:5

MOVIES *to watch*

Awakenings
starring Robin Williams
and Robert DeNiro
(1990, Rated PG-13)

The Doctor
starring William Hurt
(1991, Rated PG-13)

One True Thing
starring Renee Zellweger, Meryl Streep,
and William Hurt
(1998, Rated PG-13)

12 [Preparing for a Lifetime of Success]

MANY OF LIFE'S failures are people who did not realize
how close they were to success when they gave up.

[THOMAS ALVA EDISON¹]

f there's any piece of advice I can offer as we near the end of this book, it's this: don't give up now! I know from personal experience that the benefits and riches of intercultural marriage far outweigh the frustrations.

Thomas Alva Edison, the inventor of the lightbulb and many other modern marvels, was once asked by a reporter: "How did it feel to fail 2,000 times as you were trying to invent the lightbulb?"

Edison replied, "I didn't fail 2,000 times. I invented the lightbulb in 2,001 steps."[2]

What was the difference between Edison's attitude and the reporter's?

Perspective

One of the most challenging aspects of intercultural marriage is keeping a long-term perspective even when the immediate circumstances seem to hold only hurt, disappointment, and frustration. Those who achieve success in *any* marriage are those who offer forgiveness, show grace, and possess a willingness to see the tough times through.

My goal for this book has been to provide you with informative stories, practical tools, and biblical principles to help you overcome obstacles and achieve happiness and success in your intercultural marriage. If certain advice resonates with you and is helpful to you, please take it; if not, then it may not apply to your specific situation. Just as no two individuals are exactly the same, no two couples will navigate precisely the same marital journey.

My prayer is that, through the personal stories and interview results I've shared, you've been encouraged in your commitment to build a positive, God-honoring, and fulfilling marriage partnership. God loves you deeply, and He has a specific purpose and plan for your life. He has set out certain goals for you to accomplish through your intercultural marriage that you could not accomplish in any other way. You and I have the exciting privilege of fulfilling our divine purpose through this adventure of intercultural marriage.

In Jeremiah 29:11, God says, "For I know the plans that I have for you, plans for welfare and not for calamity to give you a future and a hope." His plans include blessings and hope for your marriage and your future.

Crucial Factors for Success

Studies show that the most fulfilled intercultural couples are those who dedicate themselves to loving and serving each other, living a life committed to God, setting and achieving goals, and reaching out to others. The intercultural couples that I've interviewed also have listed a variety of other elements that they consider vital to marital success, including:

- a true, personal relationship with Jesus Christ
- a strong commitment to the marriage
- open communication
- patience
- kindness
- honesty
- faithfulness
- a willingness to sacrifice one's personal preferences for the sake of the other

- sensitivity to each other's needs

- a positive attitude toward each other's cultures and families

- flexibility

- adaptability

- the sharing of common dreams, goals, and interests

- a spirit of adventure

- a sense of humor

- a willingness to learn each other's languages and cultural ways

- verbally building each other up rather than tearing each other down

- the dedication to stay in the marriage and work out problems when times get tough

Make it a point to sit down with a pen and paper and think honestly about your fiancé or spouse with regard to the above categories. Take notes. How does your loved one fit (or not fit) into each category? Be honest; it won't help either of you if you gloss over problems at this point in your relationship. No person is perfect; all of us have strengths and weaknesses, and it's important for you to be aware of the strengths and weaknesses of both yourself and your significant other.

Does your loved one have a personal relationship with Christ? Is he patient? Does she know any of your language at all—and does she seem interested in learning it? Does he like your culture, or does he tend to make negative comments about it? Is she a positive and encouraging person, or does she have a critical, nagging spirit? You should be able to recognize at least a few areas that suggest a possible weakness or "red flag." Write each of these down and find an emotionally neutral time to discuss your concerns with your fiancé or spouse. Everyone has weaknesses that can be turned into strengths with the Lord's help. Having the foresight and the wisdom to discuss these issues now will greatly improve your marriage down the road.

Miguel, who was from Chile, didn't try to disguise his contempt for American culture. His American wife, Carol, suffered as a result. Miguel "didn't like its politics; he criticized its work ethic; he found Americans to be rude, classless, money-hungry, and superficial. . . . His most devastating put-down to his wife was always, 'You're acting like a typical American.' Carol knew her country was less than perfect, but it was hers to criticize, hers to hate at times, not his! She took his criticisms personally, as criticisms of herself. . . . His antipathy toward everything American and her resentment of that criticism was a constant thorn in their marriage."[3]

In contrast, Mehdi and Daniele admired and appreciated each other's cultures. Daniele loved the exotic beauty of Morocco, Mehdi's home country. After the couple moved there, Daniele felt a kinship with the simplicity of life, the kindness, and the generosity of the Moroccan people, who helped her adjust to life in a new country. Mehdi also was fascinated by Daniele's home country of Belgium. He loved European art and culture, and he willingly accompanied his wife to Belgium to visit her family and spend time with her friends.[4] Clearly, couples like Mehdi and Daniele have a much higher likelihood of marital longevity and happiness than couples like Miguel and Carol.

In addition to the factors already listed, I have found the principles below to be indispensable for nurturing a successful intercultural marriage. They will provide you with a powerful framework of support when you face rough patches during your marital journey.

Be Ready to Make Sacrifices

Recently, I sat down and talked with a friend about some of the changes that have occurred in my life and in my marriage over the past year. My husband and I have put in offers on two homes, but we felt a lack of peace about both and ended up not purchasing either one. We were forced to go back to the drawing board and begin looking all over again, which was not an easy decision to make.

In addition, we recently found out that we are expecting our first child. We are absolutely thrilled about this new development in our lives, but it is requiring us to make some important financial decisions and cutbacks in our spending. In addition, it has affected my work and writing schedule and has given me a reason to stop, reflect, and pray about my values, my priorities, my marriage, my writing career, and my family.

As I talked with my friend, I told her that the process of pressing on in intercultural marriage often feels like taking "three steps forward, two steps back." Sometimes processes and decisions that seem so simple for other couples to make, like buying a home, become a long, emotional, and drawn-out ordeal for intercultural couples, and no one can pinpoint the precise reasons why. Divergent values, worldviews, priorities, different ways of making decisions, varying attitudes toward money, and more can make it difficult for intercultural couples to agree on an outcome that is mutually satisfying. Intercultural marriages can feel like much more work, and can require much more personal sacrifice, than non-intercultural partnerships.

But this line of thinking can be unproductive. I meet just as many non-intercultural couples who face disillusionment and frustration as I do intercultural couples. I know just as many same-culture couples who have divorced as I do intercultural couples—in fact, probably more. Part of the difference may be that intercultural couples usually expect to have cultural and communication issues as part of the fabric of their marriages, so they prepare to deal with those issues from the beginning and commit themselves more deeply to the relationship. Same-culture couples often don't expect to have issues related to communication, intimacy, money, child rearing, and more, so they may not be prepared to deal with conflicts on these issues.

Even with the process of taking three steps forward and two steps back, the bottom line is this: when we look back over the seven years of our marriage, we can see that we have moved forward. We have made progress! The process of working through our differences by God's grace, painful though it may have been, has made us more mature, stronger, and more flexible people. We've had to depend on the Lord to provide the light for every step that we have ventured to take. The Lord has used these circumstances in our lives to remind us that everything happens "'not by might nor by power, but by My Spirit,' says the Lord of hosts" (Zechariah 4:6).

Consider Your Marriage Your Homeland

Many intercultural spouses, especially those who have left their home, family, and friends to move to a foreign culture, begin to consider their marriage their new "homeland"—a haven of love, safety, and security.

Rani, a woman from Malaysia, says: "When I married Sune [who is Swedish], I left my family. This is one of the reasons they objected and cried at the time of my marriage; they knew they were losing me more than if I had married someone of my own kind. But it was my own choice and it is my obligation. My marriage has become my homeland; Sune and my children come first."[5]

Rani, I, and many others would agree that **creating a marriage that stands the test of time is not simple**. Yet leaving our families and friends and cleaving to another person is part of the covenant marriage relationship that God created and set forth in Scripture. Staying together for better and for worse, for richer and for poorer, requires God's supernatural strength and protection. If you're not already praying for that in your marriage, today would be a great day to begin!

One author notes that intercultural couples' commitment to their marriages is often strengthened by pride. She writes, "Many of these marriages have taken place against the advice of family or friends. . . . [The spouses] need to prove to everyone (sometimes themselves included) that they made the right decision. They don't want to admit that they might have made a mistake—that everyone else might have been right—and face the spoken or implied 'I told you so's' back home. So when faced with the prospect of marital breakdown, they have another try at working it out."[6]

Intercultural couples tend to form a unique bond—a special identity together that is quite different from the identity of each individual. This bond also provides couples with an impetus to stay together. Dugan Romano writes, "There might also be a reluctance to give up the new identity, the uniqueness the couple acquired through the marriage. It's hard to go back to being just like everyone else, especially for those who need to be different, who perhaps were escaping from something they didn't like in their own culture by marrying out of it. Often the same motives that led them into the marriage in the first place keep them working at it when the relationship goes sour."[7]

I love my husband; I enjoy our marriage; I feel that we have a joyful and God-honoring partnership. I have invested 100 percent of my time and energy into our marriage and have made many sacrifices to make my marriage work. Yes, there have been many times when I could have turned my back and walked away from my marriage (and there have been times when I felt like doing so), but God gave me the grace and wisdom not to do that. Since the Lord has specifically given me a ministry to intercultural couples, I feel called to be an example to other women. I want my life to be a picture of commitment, submission, and love in marriage, just as Christ is submitted to His Father and committed to loving His bride, the church.

Be Willing to Give and Take

One aspect that contributes to the success of intercultural couples is the willingness to take turns living in each other's cultures. My dear Brazilian friend, Liliam, came to the States from her home country to attend seminary in Dallas. While there, she met and married an American friend of mine, Jason. The couple lived in the States for several years and had a daughter, Gabriela. Liliam continued to adjust to the culture and language. At times, being away from her family and friends was a struggle, as it is for most people who leave home and move to a different country. Liliam was also faced with the illness of her father and mother, both of whom were diagnosed with cancer around the same time.

After graduating from seminary, Liliam and Jason lived in the States for a few more years. Over time, however, they felt the Lord leading them to return to Brazil to do ministry. They

moved there several years ago and now have an exciting ministry called Mobilizing Brazil, through which they train and send
out Brazilians to do missions in other countries. They now have
two daughters. I've been blessed to know them and to see God
lead them on their special intercultural marriage journey.

When Catalin first asked me to marry him, I assumed that
I would move to Romania and that as a couple we would work
for the orphan ministry that enabled us to meet. Instead,
Catalin opted to move to the States because he would have better opportunities to attend college and work here.

However, we still talk occasionally about the possibility of
moving to Romania, either for a short period of time or long-
term. I admit that, since I now feel comfortably settled in our
life here and I'm used to our marriage routine, the idea of moving to Romania is scarier for me than it once was. I love my
husband's family, I love the country, I love the language, and I
love the people. But after seeing the transition that my husband has gone through, it's tougher to consider putting myself in that situation, especially with children. I would be the
foreigner, the one left out. I would be the one who would have
to make the extra effort to reach out to people because they
might not feel quite as comfortable around me. And while my
husband speaks brilliant English, my Romanian is not even
close! However, because Catalin made the sacrifice of leaving
his homeland and family for me, I feel that I should be willing
to do the same for him if the situation should arise.

Keep a Positive Attitude

The most crucial factor for success is keeping a positive attitude about your spouse and your marriage. At times, doing
so will require deep dependence on the Lord through prayer.
Part of honoring your spouse is treating that person with love
and respect even when you don't feel like it.

The most successful couples I interviewed were optimistic
people who had a positive outlook on life and felt confident about
the way they were living their lives. They felt that their marriages
were special, and they worked hard to keep their relationships
happy and healthy. They prayed together and were committed

to having homes that were founded on the principles of God's Word. They were quick to name all of the benefits they had gained from their marriages, and they were committed to giving back to others. They were flexible and tolerant with their spouses and gave them room to grow and change.

As you continue to pursue your intercultural marriage, my prayer is that you'll reflect on the principles you've gleaned from this book and return to it often for guidance on particular topics. If you have comments or questions, please visit my Web site at www.marriageleap.com or e-mail me at marla_alupoaicei @yahoo.com.

Blessings to you!

QUOTES *for   reflection*

Blessed is the man who listens to me,
Watching daily at my gates,
Waiting at my doorposts.
● **Proverbs 8:34**

He who gives attention to the word will find good,
And blessed is he who trusts in the Lord.
● **Proverbs 16:20**

Jesus said, "Truly I say to you, if you have faith the
size of a mustard seed, you will say to this mountain,
'Move from here to there,' and it will move;
and nothing will be impossible to you."
● **Matthew 17:20**

Now faith is the assurance of things hoped for, the conviction of things not seen. . . . And without faith it is impossible to please Him, for he who comes to God must believe that He is and that He is a rewarder of those who seek Him.
●Hebrews 11:1, 6

All these died in faith, without receiving the promises, but having seen them and having welcomed them from a distance, and having confessed that they were strangers and exiles on the earth. For those who say such things make it clear that they are seeking a country of their own. And indeed if they had been thinking of that country from which they went out, they would have had opportunity to return. But as it is, they desire a better country, that is, a heavenly one. Therefore God is not ashamed to be called their God; for He has prepared a city for them.
●Hebrews 11:13–16

So then you are no longer strangers and aliens, but you are fellow citizens with the saints, and are of God's household, having been built on the foundation of the apostles and prophets, Christ Jesus Himself being the corner stone.
●Ephesians 2:19–20

MOVIES *to watch*

Remember the Titans
starring Denzel Washington
and Will Patton
(2000, Rated PG)

Something New
starring Sanaa Lathan
and Simon Baker
(2006, Rated PG-13)

Sweet Home Alabama
starring Reese Witherspoon, Josh Lucas,
and Patrick Dempsey
(2002, Rated PG-13)

[NOTES]

Chapter 1: Discovering the Joys and Benefits of Intercultural Marriage

1. Mignon McLaughlin, Wisdom Quotes, http://www.wisdomquotes.com/001367.html.
2. Dugan Romano, *Intercultural Marriage: Promises & Pitfalls*, 3rd ed. (Boston: Nicholas Brealey Publishing, 2008), 169–170.
3. Ibid., 170.
4. Kim Baumann, "Kaleidoscopes," in *Breaking Convention with Intercultural Romances: Personal Accounts*, ed. Dianne Dicks (Freedom, CA: The Crossing Press, 1995), 16.
5. Oliver Wendell Holmes, The Quotations Page, http://www.quotationspage.com/quote/26186.html.

Chapter 2: Understanding Intercultural Marriage Models and Stages

1. Dave Meurer, Marriage Missions International, http://www.marriagemissions.com/quotes-that-teach-marriage-message-311.
2. Leo Tolstoy, The Quotations Page, http://www.quotationspage.com/quote/35235.html.
3. Dugan Romano, *Intercultural Marriage: Promises & Pitfalls*, 3rd ed. (Boston: Nicholas Brealey Publishing, 2008), 8.
4. Ibid., 24.
5. "*Hotel Rwanda*," The Internet Movie Database, http://www.imdb.com/title/tt0395169.
6. Tamula Drumm, "Mixed Marriages: Why Expats Marry Foreigners and Then What Happens," TransitionsAbroad.com, http://www.transitionsabroad.com/publications/magazine/0107/mixed_marriages.shtml.
7. Romano, 11–12.
8. Ibid., 9.

9. Ibid., 9–10.

10. –13. The four intercultural marriage model diagrams are drawn from Romano, *Intercultural Marriage: Promises & Pitfalls*, 162–65.

14. David and Vera Mace, as quoted at the Marriage Missions International Web site, http://www.marriagemissions.com/quotes-that-teach-marriage-message-311.

15. Dr. Gary Chapman, *The Four Seasons of Marriage* (Wheaton, IL: Tyndale House, 2005), xii.

16. Chapman, 22.

17. Chapman, 34.

18. Chapman, 51.

19. Chapman, 10.

20. Chapman, 69–164.

Chapter 3: Surviving (and Enjoying) Your Engagement, Wedding, and Honeymoon

1. Sue Patton Thoele, from *Courage to Be a Stepmom*, Notable Quotes, http://www.notable-quotes.com/h/honeymoons_quotes.html.

2. Dugan Romano, *Intercultural Marriage: Promises & Pitfalls*, 3rd ed. (Boston: Nicholas Brealey Publishing, 2008), 19–21.

3. "Sobering Advice for Anyone Contemplating a Cross-Cultural Marriage," http://www.larabell.org/cross.html.

4. Ibid.

5. Rebecca R. Kahlenberg, "The I Do's and Don'ts of Intercultural Marriage," http://www.interfaithfamily.com/relationships/interracial_and_intercultural_relationships/The_I_Dos_and_Donts_of_Intercultural_Marriage.shtml?rd=1.

Chapter 4: Building Strong Verbal and Nonverbal Communication Skills

1. George Bernard Shaw, www.workinghumor.com.

2. Art Lucero, "And Two Shall Become One: Merging Two Racial Cultures in Christian Love," in *Just Don't Marry One: Interracial Dating, Marriage, and Parenting*, ed. George A. Yancey and Sherelyn Whittum Yancey (Valley Forge, PA: Judson Press, 2002), 134.

3. Federico Fellini, as quoted by Dugan Romano in *Intercultural Marriage: Promises & Pitfalls*, 3rd ed. (Boston: Nicholas Brealey Publishing, 2008), 125.

4. "Sobering Advice for Anyone Contemplating a Cross-Cultural Marriage," http://www.larabell.org/cross.html.

5. Gary Chapman, *The Five Love Languages* (Chicago: Northfield Publishing, 1995).

6. Ernest Hemingway, Wisdom Quotes, http://www.wisdomquotes.com/cat _communication.html.

7. Lisa Kirk, ThinkExist.com, http://en.thinkexist.com/quotes/Lisa_Kirk.

8. Man Keung Ho, as quoted by Dugan Romano in *Intercultural Marriage: Promises & Pitfalls*, 3rd ed. (Boston: Nicholas Brealey Publishing, 2008), 126–127.

9. Dorothy Tennov, *Love and Limerence: The Experience of Being in Love*, 2nd ed. (Lanham, MD: Scarborough House, 1999).

10. Merrita Tumonong, "Intercultural Marriage: Compromise & Commitment," http://www.cccwmich.org/CounselorArchive.php?action=expand&ID=19.

11. Emerson Eggerichs, *Cracking the Communication Code* (Nashville: Thomas Nelson, 2007), 11.

12. Emerson Eggerichs, *Love and Respect* (Nashville: Thomas Nelson, 2004), 210–211.

Chapter 5: Understanding Faith and Values

1. William Hazlett, as quoted by Dugan Romano in *Intercultural Marriage: Promises & Pitfalls*, 3rd ed. (Boston: Nicholas Brealey Publishing, 2008), 33.

2. Romano, 33.

3. "Value," YourDictionary.com, http://www.yourdictionary.com/value.

4. G. Shelling and J. Fraser-Smith, *In Love But Worlds Apart* (Bloomington, IN: Authorhouse, 2008), 60–61.

5. Romano, 33.

6. Ibid.

7. David C. Pollock and Ruth E. Van Reken, *Third Culture Kids: The Experience of Growing Up Among Worlds* (Boston: Nicholas Brealey Publishing, 2001), 31.

8. Ibid., 40–41.

9. Ibid., 41.

10. Romano, 35–36.

11. Romano, 36.

12. Marriage Missions, "Intercultural Marriage: Is My Way the Right Way?" see http://www.marriagemissions.com/intercultural-marriages-assump tionsmy-way-the-right-way.

13. Poem by Alex Graham James, quoted in Pollock and Van Reken, *Third Culture Kids*, 37–38.

Chapter 6: A Biblical Look at Intercultural Marriage

1. Harlan Miller, Notable Quotes, http://www.notable-quotes.com/m/miller _harlan.html.

2. "Can you provide insight into biblical teaching on interracial marriages?" Bible.org at http://www.bible.org/qa.php?qa_id=491.

3. "Loving v. Virginia," Microsoft Encarta Online Encyclopedia 2008, http://encarta.msn.com © 1997–2008 Microsoft Corporation. All Rights Reserved. See http://encarta.msn.com/encyclopedia_762504597/Loving _v_Virginia.html.

4. John Piper, *A Godward Life: Book Two* (New York: Multnomah, 1999).

5. Woodrow Wyatt, Romantic Lyrics, http://www.romantic-lyrics.com/love quotes12.shtml.

Chapter 7: Getting a Grip on Time

1. Joel Crohn, Ph.D., *Mixed Matches: How to Create Successful Interracial, Interethnic, and Interfaith Relationships* (New York: Ballantine Books, 1995), 79.

2. Ibid., 79.

3. Chart adapted from Joel Crohn, Ph.D., *Mixed Matches*, 79.

4. Dugan Romano, *Intercultural Marriage: Promises and Pitfalls*, 2nd ed. (Yarmouth, ME: Intercultural Press, Inc., 2001), 65.

5. Crohn, 80.

6. Romano, 65.

7. Ibid., 66.

8. Crohn, 80.

9. Romano, 67.

10. Ernest Thompson Seton, *The Gospel of the Redman*, as quoted by Ken Gire in *The Reflective Life* (Colorado Springs, CO: Chariot Victor Publishing, 1998), 19–20.

11. Edward Hall, *The Dance of Life* (New York: Anchor Books, 1983), 146, 163, 181.

12. *Dead Poets Society*, "Final Script," screenplay by Tom Schulman (Studio, 1989), http://www.peterweircave.com/dps/script.html.

13. Romano, 67.

Chapter 8: Avoiding Food Fights: Coming to Terms with Food and Mealtime Issues

1. Dugan Romano, *Intercultural Marriage: Promises and Pitfalls*, 2nd ed. (Yarmouth, ME: Intercultural Press, Inc., 2001), 46.

2. James Beard, The Quotations Page, http://www.quotationspage.com/quote/33518.html.

3. Joel Crohn, Ph.D., *Mixed Matches: How to Create Successful Interracial, Interethnic, and Interfaith Relationships* (New York: Ballantine Books, 1995), 57–62.

4. George Miller, "Laughter . . . The Best Medicine," http://www.csmngt.com /food_quotations.htm.

5. "Good Food Ends with Good Talk," Foodminds Blog, http://foodminds. blogspot.com/2005/09/food-quotations.html.

6. "Weird Food and Strange Food from Around the World," Weird-Food.com, http://www.weird-food.com.

7. Fanny Fern, "Laughter . . . The Best Medicine," http://www.csmngt .com/food_quotations.htm.

8. Romano, 48–49.

9. George Meredith, "Laughter . . . The Best Medicine," http://www. csmngt.com/food_quotations.htm.

Chapter 9: Managing Your Finances

1. Henry Fielding, The Quote Garden, "Quotations about Money," http:// www.quotegarden.com/money.html.

2. Real Families, "Managing Family Finances While Protecting Your Marriage," Real Answers, http://realfamiliesrealanswers.org/?page_id=60.

3. Generous Giving, Frequently Asked Questions, http://www. generousgiving.org/page.asp?sec=43&page=624.

4. Brenda Lane Richardson, Guess Who's Coming to Dinner (Berkeley, CA: Wildcat Canyon Press, 2000), 69–70.

5. Dugan Romano, Intercultural Marriage: Promises & Pitfalls, 3rd ed. (Boston: Nicholas Brealey Publishing, 2008), 85.

6. Joel Crohn, Ph.D., Mixed Matches: How to Create Successful Interracial, Interethnic, and Interfaith Relationships (New York: Ballantine Books, 1995), 205.

7. Gloria Steinem, Wisdom Quotes, http://www.wisdomquotes.com/002478 .html.

8. Generous Giving, Frequently Asked Questions, http://www. generousgiving.org/page.asp?sec=43&page=585.

Chapter 10: Rearing Your Children

1. Elizabeth Stone, Wisdom Quotes, http://www.wisdomquotes.com/001739. html.

2. Dugan Romano, Intercultural Marriage: Promises & Pitfalls, 3rd ed. (Boston: Nicholas Brealey Publishing, 2008), 109.

3. Terri Knudsen, "My Family and Other Foreigners," in Breaking Convention with Intercultural Romances: Personal Accounts, ed. by Dianne Dicks (Freedom, CA: The Crossing Press, 1995), 239–240.

4. Ibid., 240–241.

5. Susan K. Perry, "Maryam and Me," in Breaking Convention with Intercultural Romances: Personal Accounts, 166–168.

6. Anne Frank, Wisdom Quotes, http://www.wisdomquotes.com/002077. html.

7. George Santayana, Wisdom Quotes, http://www.wisdomquotes.com /003611.html.

Chapter II: Dealing with Illness and Grief

1. The Quote Garden, see http://www.quotegarden.com/grief.html.

2. Dugan Romano, *Intercultural Marriage: Promises & Pitfalls*, 3rd ed. (Boston: Nicholas Brealey Publishing, 2008), 140.

3. Ibid., 156.

4. Joel Crohn, Ph.D., *Mixed Matches: How to Create Successful Interracial, Interethnic, and Interfaith Relationships* (New York: Ballantine Books, 1995), 34.

5. Dr. Elisabeth Kübler-Ross, *On Death and Dying* (New York: Scribner, 1997).

6. Art and Sue Kinsler, as quoted by Lawrence Driskill in *Cross-Cultural Marriages and the Church: Living the Global Neighborhood* (Pasadena, CA: Hope Publishing House, 1995), 53– 54.

7. G. Shelling and J. Fraser-Smith, *In Love But Worlds Apart* (Bloomington, IN: Authorhouse, 2008), 37–38.

8. Ibid., 38.

Chapter 12: Preparing for a Lifetime of Success

1. Thomas Alva Edison, Wisdom Quotes, http://www.wisdomquotes.com /cat_success.html.

2. Heart 'N Souls, "Moral of This Story," http://www.heartnsouls.com /stories/i/s862.shtml.

3. Dugan Romano, *Intercultural Marriage: Promises & Pitfalls*, 3rd ed. (Boston: Nicholas Brealey Publishing, 2008), 179.

4. Ibid.

5. Ibid., 175.

6. Ibid., 173.

7. Ibid.

Seven Reasons Why God Created Marriage

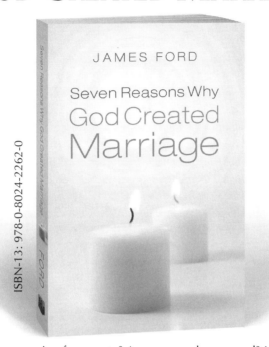

ISBN-13: 978-0-8024-2262-0

Have you been praying for a mate? Are you newly engaged? Have you recently embarked upon the journey of marriage with the love of your life? Marriage is a wonderful thing and it is without question a part of God's plan for many. So what is this thing called marriage and what are some of the foundational things you need to know as you anticipate growing old with your mate? Pastor James Ford, a seasoned marriage counselor, walks readers through the Bible and shows them seven purposes for which God created marriage. This exploration will reveal timeless truths upon which readers can build a solid foundation and strengthen th pillars of their marriage, reaping the benefits God intended along the way.

1-800-678-8812 • MOODYPUBLISHERS.COM

WHAT'S SUBMISSION GOT TO DO WITH IT?

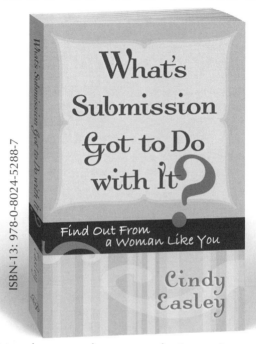

Much writing about complementary roles in marriage treats the subject theoretically. But how does this actually work in the give-and-take of real marriages, with flawed husbands and flawed wives? What about marriages where the wife out-earns the husband, or has a powerful position outside the home? Scripture says that wives are to respect their husbands. When does "submission" cross the line into destructive co-dependency? Drawing from in-depth interviews, as well as Scripture and her own story, author and speaker Cindy Easley takes a candid, sometimes humorous, and always helpful look at what it means to submit in 21st-century marriages.

1-800-678-8812 • MOODYPUBLISHERS.COM